BABEL

In remembrance
Of
Debbie Blankenship

PATTI SMITH

BABEL

G. P. PUTNAM'S SONS · NEW YORK

Copyright © 1974, 1975, 1976, 1977, 1978
by Patti Smith

All rights reserved. This book, or parts thereof, must not be reproduced in any form
without permission.

Published simultaneously in Canada by Longman Canada Limited, Toronto.

SBN: 399-12000-9 (hard cover)
SBN: 399-12102-1 (soft cover)

Library of Congress Cataloging in Publication Data

Smith, Patti.
  Babel.

I. Title.
PS3569.M53787B3   818'.5'409   77-20286

PRINTED IN THE UNITED STATES OF AMERICA

Third Impression

*this book is dedicated
to the future*

contents

I. RADIO ETHIOPIA

notice

"beauty will be convulsive or not at all."
Nadja

fade in...a field...tresses of h/air wave...the extreme and shift-
ing train of dreams. the 14 stations evoke 14 stills from the
archives of the forbidden cinema-that which is not yet
shot...that which has no perceivable die/rection.

the sound track: 14 movements/a riot of radios
the hero: the runner

heroine: the artist. the premier mistress writhing in a garden
graced w/highly polished blades of grass...release (ethiopium)
is the drug...an animal howl says it all...notes pour into the
caste of freedom...the freedom to be intense...to defy social or-
der and break the slow kill monotony of censorship. to break
from the long bonds of servitude-ruthless adoration of the
celestial shepherd. let us celebrate our own flesh-to embrace
not ones race mais the marathon-to never let go of the fiery
sadness called desire.

all honor goes to the runner who would still seek glory in the
heart of failure. all honor goes to the guardian of ritual as he
caresses the land with the entrails of language: witness the
birth of eve-she is rising she was sleeping she is fading in a
naked field sweating the precious blood of nodding blooms
...in the eye of the arena she blends in half in service-the
anarchy that exudes from the pores of her guitar are the cries
of the people wailing in the rushes...a riot of ray/dios...

14

ahhh let us go our separate ways together...let us gather on the summit of a cool volcano...plunge into the infinite pit in a jet spitting an ec-static dialogue of sound until the attar of our being permeates the red field...blood, tongue and new noise—a sonic dart-from deep in the heart of...

italy (the round)

for pasolini

picking thru the ruins w/ a stick. the wet leaves against my legs and the bottoms of my feet. in my pocket the silky roll of my stockings. my stomach is contracting. the stones are cold and wet. the rein of virgil and in the distance another castle, parted like the scalp of a student, by a seizure of mold. the quaaludes. the fluid muscle of the crowd. the hot lights. action as a blade that cuts another slice. history. limbs. nostalgic ruins in/ruin. the suspicious rivers and the caves of naples. a ripple in the water is another rib. floating dog. an anklet. a photograph-posthumous blank. a still from a film not shot.

observe cinema! what is kinder more flattering than images re-
leased w/ breath? a still? death frozen and flat in a dimension
of shadow and point. or the final shots of pasolini mugging
mineo in an alley. emotion surfaces on the face or a screen. the
light projects thru the pores of a face of promise. phasing fu-
ture fusion. filling veins w/ ice until one is altogether numb.

dubbed and brittle i can not speak. i am unable to read my
lines. the lights make my lids sweat and my eyes fill w/ salt. i
never saw so many tears. i seek a way out. funeral music is not
abstract. a dirge evokes wailing and weight. the film/maker is
blinded by the bright night. he has gone underground he has
gone under. somewhere a slayer goes undercover. fascist or
lover it doesn't matter. the scenes of pasolini remain even as
he is lowered. a flag of flies unfurl. over there, in the flowers,
erect fellows playmate. their sticky plumage curdles the blood
of observers.

the distress of molten cadavers. the winds shift and my nos-
trils split. the rigid triangle the bolt of the hare. now racing
now clinging to the great wave. a bright green feel. molecules
drop and accumulate in the shifting treasure box .the box tips
and the molecules slip and slide down a ramp of sight rays. i
am lying on my side within the bowels of a captive plane. the
co-pilot is exploring the cockpit-my intestines. i am attempt-
ing to poke a finger thru the pale membrane of a window. to
adorn w/ insertions a bank of corrosion. a wind screen of gy-
rating inlay. mercy god. my imagination is so dense i must
machete. the jungle thick w/ breach of promise to sleep in
peace. this potent state of grace is corrupted w/ the construc-
tion of amazing takes. photographs. stills from a scene not

shot. messages. hands. the rows of silence. the rotating hips of our lady of the latin highway. dwelling in favor in the caves of italy.

the rocksound. i am ninety feet up. attached to each foot is the deck of a ship. the mast is becoming wings. hair ribbons. the night just laughs just roars. light splinters. i've been up here before on this hot walk. the alcohol is exotic and thick w/ sugar. contraband cigarettes and hot liquors. my fingers are melting but i no longer need them. in the distance-musings, rock is the amplification of the lower head, so arranged that the whole inflorescence resounds as one blooming note.

OPERA IS TRUTH AND CARUSO IS QUEEN

a salon. a salad and cocaine as the seasoning. the white and impulsive grain that lines the sacristal and sexual throat.

the hotel de france. hard sailors from vienna. the motorcycle scores. seams bursting in leather and the aristocratic scams of the leather rider. all this exists. woman is as prehistoric as a kiss. and here is one shaking her palms at the sky. an actress of unmeasurable task shot by none save the eye of I.

the hot breath and false caresses of a fisherman digging a hook deep in the root of the neck of a heroine. she is overcome. first w/desire and then the desire not to be snuffed out. flutter of hand and lids. seven movements becoming seven stills in the archives of the forbidden cinema. that which has no perceivable direction. that which is not yet shot. the sleeve of a silk robe rolled up. the burning cotton. alcohol. she is shot up delicate, discreet. drifting in a cushion—massive and functional as a cloud. the slanted position of the maiden neo-pronto. the erect muscle, the thrust of a hip glistening w/crisco and sweat. the beads strung together w/thin strands of spittle. freeze frame. the hand of the hero—the uranian guerrilla. a minute 2-way radio. platinum antennae dotted w/eyes of sapphire. he runs his fingers along the artiface. perforated jewels pock the smooth surface of his aching palms.

he leaps. he is free and stumbling over the rocks, dehumanized by war. no ties w/the shore, he drags thru the tired halls that lead to the grande ballroom. drawings of motion. he spins and collides into a wall of sound—breaking thru the spectacle of illusion. ladies levitate. robots w/hearts of god serve and extend. the art of technology. the electric guitar is a voice as well as device. a bird in space. an oscar—sizzling sculpture yearning to be palmed.

a slow dissolve. my hands are burrowing filth. earth too, is alexander. i sup and plot and map out my territory — this earth i have been eating. i am strong and ready for the climb. i enter a ballroom littered w/oversized film cans. shots are blown on the curve of an exit. there is no way out; we are alone together. he has the eyes and and clothes of combat. we are tracked within an expansive joke — a majestic budget — a love travelogue seen by none and lived by some. rapture 7. wherein the former spectators are now the stars caught in the universe of mutual and prophetic trance.
    Regard! she is my face
    Regard! slots everywhere
    — the music is visceral
    — poem as plot

— a poem is a collection of words and mixed grill
a powerful sequence: a grey mule ejaculating and a young girl
splitting. underexposure. it is impossible to identify or deface
her.

the ping of the xylophone is not rain. transcend violin. a roof
of tears and corrogated tin. violence becomes them and he is
purple and impatient and pummeling.

the films are disintegrating, amateur, breaking into parts. the
heroine removes herself from the fading aura. in life, in lens,
they embark. the drums sound.
— its a ship
— no its a motor
— no its my heart
oxygen on my back. naked and greased. in black. my heart
beating like mad. moving thru the black box. free of adorn-
ment. the wind screams thru the tiny holes in my naked ears.

a flash vessel

print out

— note on immortality —

WITHOUT THAT INCONSIDERATE CUT
I COULD HAVE RULED THE WORLD -
WITHOUT THAT RUDE SLICE
THIS MOVIE WOULD HAVE GONE ON
FOREVER —

the horns. the relentless sounding. i want to put on wild is the
wind. looking at you. i want to cut off all my hair and take a
drug and another drug. love. monocaine. peel away my layers,
skin after skin, of translucent film.

italy. how lovely you are. and how treacherous is your make-up. i am an insect, a movie star. where are my shades and my boots i am lost. i have taken a lot of speed and i can't bear to live outside film. the radio and the waves of the sea. i'm coming down i'm throwing up. the radio says they are burning the fields. the blood of the poppies. the metallic mouth of a woman sleeping.

the actress blows kisses to pierre pa-olo rising from the sea. victim of fascists and faggots and the purity of his art. waving goodbye. the thrust of his arm. the trust of his view.

pasolini is dead. et morte. shower of petals. flower girls de-flowered. virgins skewered and devoured. film-deaths of hollywood stars runs simultaneous split screen 24 hours. vats of flesh and grape shot thru amo valves of cannons. balls of sight. falconetti advancing in a suit of turquoise armor. a tuxedo of manner. on the long beach twist men w/scales of sores for wings excreting chalone. ocean spittle and slobbering heart. picking the ruins—our pates w/a stick. our mines are going. we bleed on the sheets. diamonds, not coal, cease to exist. fuel lives! and life, like film, goes on.

the tapper extracts

one does not hold the key, he extends it

zookey, the tapper of precious blood
looks down at his mother
bending over the river
beating the clothes with a stone.
in/space the tapper extracts:
the mute procession of the twelve tribes
the rude zigernaut
a mesopotamia hotel
la taj mahal
the keeper of bees
the insatiable dreamer that totems the manor
the icing of light...
awareness is relative and anyone relating to the tapper
feels the fluids of the future flooding his veins. the
screen projects deliverance...vague silver members...the
lost years of jesus and cleopatra...tablets unearthed from
the dawn of time...searchlights over the labyrinth. the
rube flux in a vibrant twist of thread...

tapper, the extractor, ties it all together. like a
playful cat he taps the unraveling ball and sends it
out and over like a corvette over detroit landing on
the throat of the babeling son of ritual.
he cries a/men o/men.
his bodily fluids coagulate into a smooth stone
etched with the synchronizing symbols
words of power/verbs of light

songs of the valley and singers forgotten
shackles of slaves opening like laughing wounds
the shining faces of the liberation
the gentle panorama
there is no power
save the power
and the hour of commune
through zookey
the keeper
the queen and the drone
there is a sweet and distant buzzing
there is a swelling in our breath
we are in the pit of re/action
the ma/sonic key of the keeper is turning
the sky is black
the bushes are burning
the walls of the bull
the thread is unraveling
rending and splittting
and the people are rushing
like the heat of the chamber
rushing like water
like the heart of the lion
raising and shaking his paw
embracing and shaking
w/zookey the extender
standing in/space
looking down at his mother
bending over the river
and his father
working in the field.

grant

i think it was on the sabbath, the day of rest, that trouble was
invented. the creator fell asleep and dreamed. it was the first
sleep and the first dream. the dream of god. the primal pan-
dora. from the subliminal of the spirit arose monsters and art-
ists. masters and the archangel.

today is sunday and i have spent some of it with my father. the weather scares me but i like it. it's raging out. my body hurts as it always does when the weather is bad. it came quite unexpectedly. the sky went black and it was hailing in the spring. i never know what it's going to be like anymore because he doesn't tell me. it used to be he'd call and say, "it's a storm here. you'll have it in two days." or "the sun is coming." i needed no other source but the word of my guardian.

we live for a very long time in our imagination for the misfit it is the light and heady alternative. the misfit is one who is true and troubled and filled with shining blood. but for my father the irrevocable alien, there is nowhere to go, unaccepted by the real world and betrayed by the divine, he has plunged into a state of atrophy. a trophy a stationary prize. it is the junky becoming the junk the dreamer the dream. it is the masterpiece himself. a/trophy.

god sleeps. his people — devout, ambitious and correct — regard the sabbath with complete charge and submission. being of one tongue and of one mind, mindful of him, they probed him delicately. here they are devoted and bent on his day of rest and choice. their growing numbers. their telepathy. their merging energies craved house, craved test and plunger. thus they materialized the first hypodermic. thus they were able to inject their concentration into the pit of his dreaming.

thus they were made intimate with the most intimate of the spirit. it was there that man communicated with higher orders and there he learned the great secrets. babel imposed unspeakable wrath. for they had learned the secret of levitation thru communication. the secrets of god, of architecture. they became one with his spectres, his archangels, and the sounds auraying the revelation.

for him it was a day of complete escape from his social involvement with his creations, the dilemmas of good and evil and of those not able. for him it was the time of precious truth. of dream.

i imagine god jealous and crazy — ribbed in neon dayglow. he just can't believe that his people, the ants, have tapped into him through the sabbath. he had exposed himself as a result of the harmonic alchemy that existed between his dreaming and their worshipping. he could not accept that they were so connected and so he caused them disconnected. man was condemned to wander the earth like hordes of leper telephones.

a gale, 20 mile winds. the rain.

i imagine and i dream. god sleeping. my father searching. god awakes and scoops him up and embraces him. there is the father — king kong and my father — the golden one.

today i've spent some time with my father. i have watched and listened and opened w/ him. have shared his longing—his desire for perfect union. his disappointment in a destiny of wandering far from heaven. his resignation. his suffering the agony of losing his grip on the thread of dreaming. the final corrupting of his innermost dream by the invasion of the surveyors of reality.

I recognize him as the true outcast. he is lucifer the unguided light, judas the translator and barabbas the misused. so certain of gods existence he would attempt to deny, defy or seek him beyond the constricts of the law—the rock. he has backed the validity of denial because of the imperfection of man and his facts and miscalculations when dealing with the abstract.

so it is and so it has always been. I recognize a man with dark glasses, of medium height in a brown shirt. an acrobat, a runner, a factory worker and the husband of my mother.

I recognize the tower of babel as a symbol of penetration. the symbol of a moment when mans desire to be close to god was so intense that he invaded his dreams. i recognize a man whose dreams have also been invaded and truly believe there is no/one closer to god than my father.

street of the guides

those who have suffered understand suffering and thereby extend their hand. the storm that rends harm also makes fertile. blessed is the grass and herb and the tree of thorn and light.

on the street of the guides the lepers huddle. a bus passes. this vehicle is reserved for the ethiopians. tall and beautiful and unmarked save the monstrous distension of their limbs. the burden of their limbs is elephantiasis.

the lepers have pity on their brothers. the lepers have the luxury of immediate scorn, while the ethiopians must experience adoration, and then witness the observers' disintegration into slow but finite horror. the ethiopians are worshipped by the lepers. here they are magnificent athletes, saints and studs. in return the lepers are gifted with fresh rolls of linen—dressing and cover for their weeping sores. often one is presented with a crown of bright leaves. the laurels from a tournament. a hero presents his laurels to the slave of disease. the slave rests the garland on the head of the chosen and rolled.

one is leaving tonight. he had stayed on for a while in the only remaining inn, the hotel care. he was regarded as a hero there for his feats at marathon. now his legs are useless and soon he will be dead. the bus slows down and he is hoisted on. the eerie sight of a scrambling disease illuminated by the yellow street lamp fills his heart with gas. soon his heart will break, will burst into stars. his mother was scourged and his sister was scourged. but he was blessed. for them they see only his face. he is not like the others. no disease has touched him. just fate. his car losing control on a sheet of grease.

the bus slowly passes over the cobblestone street of the guides. the lepers sigh with pleasure and hail the visage of the mighty ethiopians.
their faces radiant, unmarked
their legs, covered.

rimbaud dead

he is thirty-seven. they cut off his leg. the syphilis oozes. a cream virus. a mysterious missile up the ass of an m-5. the victim suffers soul-o-caust. his face idiotic and his marvelous tongue useless, distended.

rimbaud. no more the daring young horseman of high abyssinian plateau. such ardour is petrified forever.

his lightweight wooden limb leans against the wall like a soldier leisurely awaiting orders. the master, now amputee, just lays and lays. gulping poppy tea through a straw—an opium syphon. once, full of wonder, he rose in hot pursuit of some apparition—some visage. perhaps harrar a heavy sea or dear djami abandoned in the scorched arena-aden. rimbaud rose and fell with a thud. his long body naked on the carpet. condemned to lie there at the mercy of two women stinking of piety. rimbaud. he who so worshipped control now whines and shits like a colic baby.
now appointed now basket case wallowing in rice waste. now muscular tongue now dumb never to be drunk again. save tea time when he pulls the liquid in. gasping it deludes the bloodstream. conscience abandons him. he's illuminating kneeling climbing mountains racing. now voyager now voyeur. he notes it all. very ernest surreal oar. his artificial limb lifts and presses space. limb in a vacuum.

does rimbaud beckon?

no he's gazing

in the wall is a hole. duchamp thumbprint pin light fraction. an iris opening. gradually we see the whole thing. everything opens unfolds like a breugal. it's a holiday...

it's a wedding feast...

they're roasting pigs and apples apron. the odor is rising. it's
sunday it's manet it's picnic in the grass. it's a seurat time it's
light time it's the right time for romancing for canoeing and
for dancing.

and rimbaud's limb, being so caught up, goes be-bopping out
the door into the forest through the trees—raga rag in the grass
overturning picnic baskets whizzing past churchyard gates
right in step it genuflects then aims and leaps over the scene
over the rainbow out of the canvas into space pure space—as
remote and colorless as dear arthur's face. a face made incor-

poreal full of grace. sunken eyes—those cobalt treasures
closed forever.

clenched fist relaxed wrist
his pipe turned in...

out in the garden the children are gathering.
it's not a whim. they are accurate immaculate,
as cruel as him.
they sing:
legs can't flail
cock can't ball
teeth can't bare
baby can't crawl
rimbaud rimbaud facing the wall
cold as hail dead as a doornail

sudden tears!

sohl

a cluster of glories erupted from his skull.
filled with a holy dread he opened his
chest and removed a small oval hand mirror.
ivory and crystal and perfectly wrought. he
had intended to inspect his head but instead
dwelt for several minutes on the elegant
craftsmanship of the mirror. the ivory had
a rich grain, veins, and in the center, a
crack. he knelt down and squinted so as to get
a better look. in the crack there was a garden.
it was so green that he fell down in laughter
and rolled and rolled in and over the cool
blades. the blood streamed and covered the amazing
fields. the pale glories, accustomed to worship,
reared their heads and let themselves be washed
in the ruby luxury. after several days of
rain and all traces of the man gone the
children were let free to roam and gloat in
the long fields of poppies.

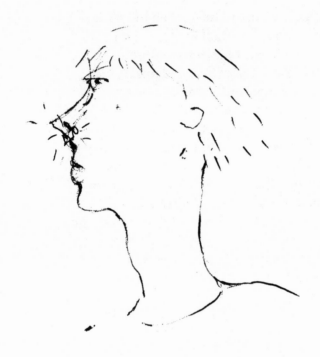

27 mai '25

neo boy

the son of a neck
rilke

everything is shit. the word art must be redefined. this is the age where everyone creates. rise up nigger take up your true place. rise up nigger the word too must be redefined. this is your arms and this is your hook. don't the black boys get shook. high asses get down. nigger no invented for the color it was made for the plague. for the royalty who have readjusted their sores. the artist. the mutant. the rock n' roll mulatto. arise new babe born sans eye-brow and tonsil. outside logic,

beyond mathematics, self-torture and poli-tricks. arise in/
health new niggers and celebrate the birth of the one. this is
your calling and this is your psalm. rise up niggers and reign
w/your instruments of fortune.

everything comes down so pasturized
everything comes down 16 degrees
they say your amplifier is too loud
turn your amplifier down
are we high all alone on our knees
memory is just hips that swing
like a clock
the past projects fantastic scenes
tic/toc tic/toc tic/toc
fuck the clock!

Time is a woman reshaping, taking watch.
she perfumes her hair w/the attar of battle
her armor is the rose cut brass of allah.
bond or bondage
that is the question
arise! the people divided are not strong enough.
arise nigger we are summoned by the panel of horns.
of the rim of horn and the space around.
spread w/hoops and hooves
and the grain of clarity/and charity
he who challenges the king
receives commune and call
trial by riddle/trial by fall
communication of the future
is not in heaven
its here man

je/hova I have
the son of time pieces it all together
the 17 jewels of the alchemist
a burning breast

Time is a myth
of gold and shit
like karat eggs easing out of goose ass
the long animal cry/woman is blessed
the perfect merging of beauty and beast
the green gas moving in like excitement
and the slip/slipping
sliding into layers of wax
red black gone and going
a woman alone in a tube of sound
resounds is resounding
a long low whine
moving thru the spine
a pelvic wind up
thru the primal arms
newboy is spawned
bald and screeching
like an eagle on a table
w/tongue preserved
coiling then flashing
a slender thread of lightning
piercing tense and shattering space
a woman gives birth to an ass and a face.

everything is shit. no i don't believe it. calligraphy glows.
inspired worms twine and emit a hairy rubbery light.
great hands twist and bend the strings and shoot high

sliming fugies thru comic neon. neo boy is born again
in the red and yellow torrents of rock n' roll shinar . . .

scrapbook green suit
standing over john
legs spread spurting gold
i was a hipster/revival
swinging chain
bending and bombing
the face of a finishing school
a fool leaning juke box
altar kneeler
action painter
misery herself writhing on a bed
of pale blue mohair
there and not there
i was several others
and i was your mother
i manufactured your nectar
and moved from your presence
to worship your radiance
baby hold the lamp
my generous equal
baby hold the lamp
on my celestial body
the bells just vomit
the hard grunts
the magical moans
w/our duty union
and our sweet detachment
baby hold the lamp
shooting arrows shooting arrows

city of glittering architecture city of endless spheres
moons of light-billowing face masks-city of minarets-
city of stars-amours-city of love and birth-of you
neo boy star of my belly.
each cry we utter is lost
if you killed ten of the people it wouldn't matter
if you save the son of a king it's worth a lot

i am your savior
i am your lover
i am several others
and i am your mother
who moves from your presence
my radiant
my eminent
epidemic

city of stars

christ! the colors
of your energies.

neo boy melts in jelly machine. the whole
thing is how he can change the scene or be
changeling. transformation is relative says
neo boy. tropical plants shiver. what can you
say about habitat that hasn't been said be-
fore? greedy children lap up radio active jew-
els spit in the dunes by algerian know-it-alls.

lilies / crowns - eyes either way
i'le / be dead

soon the gleaming bones of innocents will
scatter the sands and some enterprising old
jew will gather them up in an old leather bag
and sell them to a contact. a roman woman, a
catholic. a beautiful though childless shrew
who will rearrange the bones with all the dis-
creet adoration of a japanese boy adjusting
his weapon.

neo boy plucks up a sharp metal star and cuts
a new scene from a sheet of copper. what can
you say about habitat that hasn't been said
again? lillies crown eyes. i'll soon be dead.
condemned to total peace despite the long
chain of unspeakable horrors i carve from a
span of flat coil.

milky spirals boring in a clearing and ooze a
message significant only to happy boys cele-
brating twin births. the frolic w/buck in
miles of icing. pausing to let arrows fly from
their birthday bows. a million darts pierce
the ice forest evaporating crystal deer leap
like melting eye of butter. neo boy just nods
and laughs then slides deep in his machine
messing with the multi-colored controls and
merging with blue fish space. neon squiggles.
squirl squaggle. yes! it's neo boys electric
spaghetti calligraphy. he's just signed his
name to a perfect work of art—the sky. bones
of children and a nice winding fart blown
from the ass of neo boy—blow over the town
called bethlehem. all this shit over a town.
antidisestablishmentarianism. against the
church of england. he readjusts the dials. ev-
erything explodes then rearranges. landscape
can be recreated says neo boy proudly dis-
playing his platform—one of the most expan-
sive on the planet. every town known to man
in perfect miniature. there is harrar. there is
the white stucco arena reserved for victims of
plague and memory and abandoned space
where no one is out of place here. where only
a shapely waitress would be out of shape

here. let me out let's eat shit. neo boy has a
pain in his playing arm. must get him his gui-
tar. window breathes sigh of relief. no base-
ball thru me today. outlines pulse. its neo boy
teenage alchemist. peel your winky-dink
screens. neo boy is coming. fu-ching will at-
tempt to shake him up with victorian chink
trunks but our boy is steps ahead with all the
invisible guile of a sixteenth century jap/
immortal kamikaze divine wind assigned to
crash laughing. neo boy w/skin shimmer. yel-
low rubber tissue fingers forming crazy
mountains etched in pink florescent shad-
ows. flubber shadow. paper flowers nodding
rhyming bearing red teeth. neo boy grins and
leaps into the sea pommaded with blood. the
sticky kisses. the wet and shining lips of neo
boy slobbering on his master. the innocent
worship. the exotic mathematics. the music
of neo boy popping electric exclamation
points from wet tongue of neo boy on com-
mack spleen rack. sliding home free like
oiled baseball thanks to oil droplets on the
feathers of neo boy craning his neck to aim
sink and eat (not devour) the moon. goo-rain
la lune caught like a gas bubble in the belly
of neo boy dreaming of remarkable voyages
accursed ships frozen in dish shapes and his
crazy disgrace as he exits in a field of jazz.

city of stars city of glitter and architecture
city of endless spheres moons of light city of
lost logics city of love and birth . . .

the aquatic origins of neo boy marvelling in-
ternally, his facilities and the facility in

which he is able to project pictures. that old
pine tree glows like cinema! scores of radi-
oactive angels mugging for the camera. mug-
ging and twisting in a huge white teepee - an
erect parachute of salt frozen only a few feet
away from the young blonde pilot foaming in
the snow. his mouth filled with the seven
numb fingers and the two blue cereleum eyes
of neo boy charging down a bright green hill
drenched in armor of pale tissue. lookout sta-
dium here he comes! honey bears and gentle
beasts cheer as he rips their tormentor (shape
of an eight feet metal teethed monster) into
lurking thunder. Yay! finger mouth is advanc-
ing. Yay! metal teeth is mincing words. Yay!
neo boy wipes them all out with his atomic
dusting cloth. the miniature animals saw
horses and wavy deer frolic around the party
cake. horses leap from their porcelain skins
and the sky fills with numbers.

tired little boys have to go to bed. tired little
boys are half sleepy momma. no truths do
they know but the truths i have told them.
love and levitation nothing infrared is for-
eign. go my sleepy boys. when they do not
dream they vomit.

dog dream

have you seen
dylans dog
it got wings
it can fly
if you speak
of it to him
its the only
time dylan
cant look you in the eye

have you held
dylans snake
it rattles like a toy
it sleeps in the grass
it coils in his hand
it hums and it strikes out
when dylan cries out
when dylan cries out

have you pressed
to your face
dylans bird
dylans bird
it lies on dylans hip
trembles inside of him
it drops upon the ground
it rolls with dylan round
its the only one
who comes
when dylan comes

have you seen
dylans dog
it got wings
it can fly
when it lands
like a clown
he's the only
thing allowed
to look dylan in the eye

mirza

every race is conquering. she was killed by another of my dogs. she was already belonging to the past. she was sympathetic. beyond dignity like an extinct yet waving flower. she was lying there under the cyprus tree pouring syrup from her clock. the spring in the back of her neck was clear and sweet. supposed fresh. i don't know. i never drank nor did i pass long in those eyes as necessary to history as the glasses for a 3-D movie. this dog was sympathetic. in the remote soil of her eyes were the ruins, the arcades, the archways of history.

the dog who killed her was beaten up. mourners demanded his skin but i could not kill him. he was more wolf than dog. that idiot smile. i cut his teeth. i put him in prison. i put him out to run w/the old women. the women with rattles in their chests. lately i run with him, maybe i love him more than before. i pass for hours in those sorrowful eyes. the lore of fathers. he sits beneath the big cyprus tree. when the sky is heavy w/almonds. when the sun is beating down. when the fanwise invasion of wind whistles in his mouth he is always passing there, his eyes remote and sympathetic, resting directly on the future with the sticky sweetness of a clock.

idiot rule. the big tree fucks the small grass. tomorrow i am a tadpole, an insignificant shell. but this afternoon i pass for a very long time. dreaming and feeling a thrill to the kill of mirza. to when my young wolf dog was mad w/the projection of the human personality.

the stream

several nights after i had filed the teeth of my favorite dog i noticed the atmosphere shifting around me. i became addicted to a paste of almond meal and paregoric. i seemed to identify with everything. i was the foundation, the sticky coil of a vase. i was odorless stacks of fresh-fired plates-the cold stone of the kiln. it was impossible to work. rolling the coils was the worst. they became alive in my hand. the lovely unrelenting statues would undulate in smoke. the freshly molded huntress waved her wrists and i could discern her hips rotating sweetly under her girdle of soft wet clay. with the rope and pulley i laid her against the wall.

i was sweating and shivering and she was beckoning. i pressed my lips against her melting face; the coils of her hair squishing between my eager fingertips. i was the goddess composed of salt. the fresh deer were poking their cool snouts against me chewing my tunic and sucking my parts. i became addicted to a paste of almond meal and paregoric of humping and shattered art. my trade suffered. tourists and holy men sought vessels...souvenirs of the graced grounds where my dogs ran in packs. i suffered too. passed for hours on a bed of dust tormented w/lust for objects, doors and an intense craving for a sweet and sticky gas to blot me out. the dogs were wilder than ever. i couldn't breathe. the women noticed and had a special tea sent to me in the evenings.

on the fourth night there was a new shift. the sensation of invasion by a palpitating fist of warm light. the tea was sweet. at the bottom of the glass was a colorless grape. in a few hours it turned. i put it in the glazed bowl i had made for mirza. i had forgotten about the bowl but now it seemed to dominate the room. the bowl was a breast w/a sore and poking nipple. was a pouting mouth. was the swell of the oiled bottom of a slave. i layed on my stomach my heart pounding against the stone floor . . . my sex obliterated by objects. the bowl grew still larger. the vibrating grape split and revealed a white snake. someone had eaten a portion of it. something was alive and wriggling inside of me. my belly swelled like the cheeks of a glassblower. i couldn't move. the pains increased into the sound of wailing curses. the women entered. circled and shook their rattles. montage of trees, bowls and canine teeth. who would feed my wolf...the sting of relief won out.

i lay there for several days conscious only of the motion of my head rising, lips to a glass or a stream of powder entering my veins. one afternoon after the fever subsided i rose up w/a start. i dressed in a simple suit of cloth stuff...searched and inspected everything. the statues and larger vessels had been preserved w/wet sheets. nothing lost. everything was blooming and the air was like milk. in the clearing my wolf was lying. no one had watered her. she was a translucent coat of fur lying beneath the cyprus tree. i called for a boy to gather a syphon and a bowl that had belonged to mirza. i remembered the spring and drew from it. i had never drank from it but the waters were legendary. before us was health from which i dipped and drummed between her teeth. i felt woozy. i laid my head on the coat of my dog and we slept for a long time.

dream of rimbaud

I am a widow. could be charleville could be anywhere.
move behind the plow. the fields. young arthur lurks
about the farmhouse (roche?) the pump the artesian
well. throws green glass alias crystal broken.
gets me in the eye.

i am upstairs. in the bedroom bandaging my wound. he
enters. leans against the four-poster. his ruddy cheeks.
contemptuous air, big hands. i find him sexy as hell.
how did this happen he asks casually. too casually.
i lift the bandage. reveal my eye a bloodied mess;
a dream of Poe. he gasps.

i deliver it hard and fast. someone did it. you did it.
he falls prostrate. he weeps he clasps my knees. I grab
his hair. it all but burns my fingers. thick fox fire.
soft yellow hair. yet that unmistakable red tinge.
rubedo. red dazzle. hair of the one.

oh jesus I desire him. filthy son of a bitch. he licks
my hand. I sober. leave quickly your mother waits. he
rises. he's leaving. but not without the glance from
those cold blue eyes that shatters. he who hesitates
is mine. we're on the bed. i have a knife to his
throat. i let it drop. we embrace. i devour his scalp.
lice fat as baby thumbs. lice the skulls caviar.

oh arthur arthur. we are in abyssinia aden. making love
smoking cigarettes. we kiss. but its much more. azure.
blue pool. oil slick lake. sensations telescope, animate.
crystalline gilt. balls of colored glass exploding.
seam of berber tent splitting. openings, open as a cave,
open wider. total surrender.

doctor love

love is a vampire. the dead facts. energy undead. here in dreams he captures girls. the girls are left to their own devices. a free society observed on lividio—live video. the silvery brazen image of the collapse of pure democracy. within the confines of his modern fortress he charts the construction of the tiny female state like a sociologist over ants/bees. Just as these mad ones are able to find space w/the pearl and tray of a florentine doily, so is doctor love able to depattern their subtle intricacies into a sheet of cold logic. once he has figured them out he does away w/them.

the lighthouse in the distance is hope. no one reaches out. a girl in black silk capris bending over, sobbing. he dissects and drains until he has each one down. strange chances? nothing. these women crave organization. the reward for their therapy is extermination. love craves flaws, distinction. the challenge of the wrath and whims of a real woman. the arch of the ceiling collapses. i am in the laundry room. there i am the target of investigation. there i am the dirty linen, the kink in the machine. love is impatient to remove us. a new crop of women is arriving—raw and invigorating.

there is nothing intriguing about our group. they were rounded from one class...a sorority w/the exception of myself, a bystander. a band apart schoolgirl. they search for something inside of me. the way to turn me on. they look to switch on the least likely candidate. i've never been anything but trouble for everyone. the other girls regard me as a gram of misfortune unsettling the delicate balance of their destructive order. order here means death. the perfect circulation of their cool unit presents the proper UD flow, the food and prey of hakim love. all incentive directives point to order. order, the cruel drain. disintegration save the cells that join the cells of the undead.

ii

for a while i drew but some found out about it and i feared i'd be classified as an artist. i was afraid they would find a place for me in their society and thus perfect declare their state to the V———. their reward—the sucking of their blood. all fluids rotating in harmony within his ancient greedy veins.

i therefore stopped drawing. sometimes i slip away (like this moment) and take open my red portfolio w/the soft burlap ribbons. i like to run my hand across the skin of each drawing. they cannot classify me without evidence. a flash of sulphur and one by one they are consumed by flame. they cannot classify me as an artist. art ceases. i've stopped. i dream of escape.

4 december. love is in a bad humor. he rounds us up. he calls the role for extermination. i call to protest. i have defied order. there is nothing left of the artist. no mood of creation. the rules call for a fixed state. all eyes fix on me. he is agitated, distracted. yours is a new classification, an offshoot of sig. 101— artist. sig. 1016—mutant. it is sunday. the sabbath is observed. death begins monday. as he is reading thursday's list a man

enters. love softens. he seems to have lost interest in us. his eyes connect w/the eyes of the stranger by a thin shaft of stars. white man on a rope. he fast assigns the cook, myself, and a few remaining for friday.

finished on friday. everyone back to work. i feel so lonely like i don't belong except involuntarily. just mute, alien. the old gentleman leaves. he gives me sympathy w/his eyes. but then all visitors do, sometimes i think even love...days pass. monday's girls go. tuesday morning the old man returns. he had spent most of his life as a serf here and now, as a free man, he chooses to die here. there is a curious sense of loyalty here to love. in truth i seem the only one who wishes to leave. the spark that jetted from the visitor is dead. he is dying. escape is relative. he is about to enter love's quarters. before he does he slips a small parcel in the pocket of my trousers. the pockets are lined w/silk and i feel a high itch through my system. his hard calloused fingers smooth my thigh through the lining. the parcel jingles and fills me w/light. i understand the gift is escape. he stares at me softly, then withdraws.

no one has seen. i guess. it's difficult to assess as no one reacts to anything. their capture, their sentence, a new recipe, shine, rain, all the same. no one resents me, no one sees me. i am not even a rebel. nothing. a mutant accepted. they are even bored w/the plague but i guard my sores, i cannot accept defeat. my desire to escape mounts, tuesday's girls gone. i'm getting over-excited. beads of sweat decorate my forehead. i am a crazy car-vel. wednesday the death bells ring. the old man is dead. my blood implodes. my skin shells a mild inferno. i must keep my composure. my obsession, escape, is only slightly rattled by his death. i feel a cold dry kiss on my mouth. i inhale the va-pors of dry ice. some thing has entered me. something stirs, jets. my face is charged. bones—vibrating, electric.

doctor love has little interest in wednesday's girls. it occurred to me that had they fought or cried they may have been spared. it never seemed to cross their minds. death was listless, routine. me—i was desperate, addicted. i could not eat, just shoot pilot after pilot of my deam of escape. that night i was filled w/fever. and honor too, for the parcel (which i constantly handled like a rosary) was my connection w/a blessed future.

thursday morning was a service for the old man. i felt my duty to attend. love was not openly distressed but i felt his loss. i bent down to kiss his cold wrists. i felt his sympathetic glance. i don't know. i was so distracted, the inane pitied victim of a habitual conspiracy.

alone and pounding i was sure someone suspected. it was too quiet. there was a continuous buzzing, a drone. for a while i was sure i had been bugged. an electronic device had been embedded in my nodes and temple. thursday's girls were taken away. a trainload of fresh ones arrived. tomorrow i would die. it had to be tonight. the vampire went to his quarters for evening repaste. the cook was praying. there i was against the wall, misfit full of faith. suddenly it starts rising from my shoes. knowledge...power...i've imagined...shot and reshot this escape for days. now it's about to be realized. image: dancing nude in a munich discotheque. opening like willing scissors for the hands of men. imagination is about to be realized. pulling against action is that dangerous fear of change. survival is stronger and i decide it must be now.

love will be retiring for the evening. the full moon will serve me light. it will also make me more visible. i unwrap the parcel. it's a baby bracelet of platinum beads strung on a silver wire. dangling is a tiny gold heart and a gold key. i remove the key and slip through the yards.

the spotlights are armed toward the windows. the fear here is not escape but assassination. my heart stops. love's silhouette just above me but i keep running. the night is bright, silent. holy skies sprayed w/large stars and the moon in full rein. i reach a hedge w/an iron door. trembling i open it w/the key. within there is another hedge, high and endless like the great wall. two enormous fat black pussycats appear. massive cheshires brushing my legs. i'm afraid of them. i don't know if they're allies or enemies. i chance it. i follow them. i'm following them.

they lead me to a wall. a section of the wall has a low carved door which gives easily as i push into it. i shimmy through. it's difficult. the cats slip after me. they are an ominous pair, evils from pandora's box. little time for guilt. i wonder, i run, i run like mad. fields are immense and bright. the moon lights the sky like an eternal match. my tears contain no salt. rhymes race through my feet, pounding black beat of my heart, black cat black bat. it's true there is a shadow stretched across the luxurious face of pie. i run i run. i pray the peasants won't return me. i pray i've escaped forever from the fortress of doctor love. i imagine the women in their starched linens, heads shaven, assigned and numbered, punctured and drained. i imagine the boy, opal, crying and siphoning the metallic substance from the ritual caldron into large silver vats. here and there picking out hairs and clots and small insects. i run i run, and then I see them. through the trees. horses. white red and spotted. one is waiting. a hard miniature appaloosa w/long yellow hair. i leap on her, a graceless but true movement and i ride like hell.

iii

now i've lost control. i become someone else's point of view. the eye of the camera pulls back. i am merely a movement in a long shot of horses, fields and trees. i am riding a predestined escape route. i understand i am the (escape)goat. i have unleashed two huge black candlesticks onto the altar of illusion. the fiery bat opens her wings of raging chiffon. soft frame of sky smoky yellow sky dawn and ground. lateral tracking. a castle. a woman w/long chestnut hair waits like a statue to be unveiled. her form caressed w/layers of silky flame. suddenly her face lights up and she brushes her hair.

voiceover: *she was happy. she was queen. she who devours the suckling pig and the mutant folds. she waited, sometimes forever, for one perfect flaw to arrive. to carve and suck and bless. coming to her was the jewel she had craved. was the knob in the canvas. doctor love sent a wave of lush fruit through her delicate glistening spine of crystal. his hand gently squeezed the rare compote of her spleen. i was entering the scene. she was happy. his queen. all too pleased that her wait was not in/vein.*

AFTER/WORDS

i was led into a miniature amphitheatre of white porcelain. the
floor tiles buzzing like kinetic sculpture, waving like the color
patterns of Vasereley. columns formed a large rectangle. dead
center was a marble slab fitted w/a raft of leather. they laid her
on the table. a green cone descended through the skylight, a
draft of roses through the open window her costume was cov-
ered w/petals. every woman in history she was, and every
womb in venture. i looked in the mirror. i gave birth to alex-
ander, i was his lover. war paint formed on my face, ochre and
lavender slashes. the woman w/the chestnut mane stood over
her. her delicate hands worked small miracles. slender cel-
luloid tubes were swiftly inserted into the pores of the victim,
a virgin. the tubes were tentacles melding w/her veins her
dreams and deeper into the virginal light, the pool beneath
memory. a ruby flux where no words were formed. the queen
was a goddess strapping to herself a love mechanism—a de-
vice designed for penetration. a pointed cylinder of jeweler's
plat. i held back as long as i could. i was the throne she was
mounting. i was the seed of destiny, the conceit of reign. first
would be the poke, the light, and then the kiss. a flood of
steam and wire released. i could not resist her face was con-
necting w/my own. the rush and hiss of a mammal going un-
der.

—what do you want out of me? she said
—undulating beneath her I cried - lust!
—what do you want out of me, I asked her.
—language, she said, language.

II. ALIEN TO ALIEN

munich

it was all a dream. i hadn't washed my hair for forty days for forty nights. hennae locks hung heavy and greasy about my shoulders. i laid back and the woven mass stenched across the pillow, porous and sad. the blue light made my hands look transparent. the pink and yellow lights were sucked up by my greedy braids. a faded shot of falconetti beseeched me. typed over her grainy yeux were old words partly clouded by dying palms.

maria fake
renee falconetti
i'm mad for you
your death in life
in film as jeanne
darc of light
dry yellow palm
crown of thorns
line of blood

tier du sange
that circle circles
your morphine eyes
raccoon raccoon
your morphine eyes
like two wet balls
you got balls
you got balls

a latin cry, so far on the wall;

her head shaven, etched with language, was a stark delica-
cy—a way out. i pulled myself up. my night shirt was stained.
everything was caked with skin and sweat. the head of my
lady consumed, shined. i rose with effort, filled with joy. one
seized with a plan. i moved toward the wall. the tie that binds
us together was fever. i did a turn. i was looking for scissors
but i was immediately distracted. i moved toward the wall. i
reached out and smoothed my hand across the grain. it was
georgian, eighteenth century. a writing desk dominated by
tiny arches and secret compartments. in one was a passport. in
one was a tower, a miniature of the ziggurat of babel and a
sapphire of india. red and black. i pulled the cloth from the
window. the light flooded the room with such urgency that i
started laughing. the stone had a star in its navel. i played with
its nostrils, lubricated them with stardust, then moved over to
my other things and other times. an agfa lupe 8X for magnify-
ing sections of photographs. pociao-bonn. richard sohl-new
york. brian jones in black and white banquet. a barbarian in
scotland. i was coming in focus. i found the scissors. my locks
fell in clumps on the floor. i tore thru the drawers. all this ac-
tion in a few seconds. a rubber stamp, tattoo ink and numbers.
double sevens shone from my cropped skull like a radiant
scar. i felt lucky, completely new and cut off from the posses-
sive grip of my previous existence. long periods of insomnia
bouts with fever and death small and breath/taking.

it took a long time for me to clean myself because the heat in
the shower made me dizzy. i leaned against the tiles and
stretched out my left arm. i pressed my palm hard against the
enclosure and very slowly, so i wouldn't notice, i'd spicket the
water pure froid—cold as you can get it. i had the urge to shit
voltaire style, so i stood and pushed and squeezed my eyes un-
til the long clay turd drooped and dropped and hit the por-
celain shaft. i watched it slowly make its way down the drain.
i washed my feet in the white bowl, dried and dressed myself

in a fresh suit of linen. there were several hundred pounds in the dresser as well as sheafs of uncut francs. there were no marks. everything fresh. mint. i unrolled my scabbard. in a scarf of red leather i wrapped the money, my sebsi and the first book that filled me with ecstasy. once again fever saw it dominate my senses. once again i had successfully escaped its limitless boundaries. i leaped thru the frame into the canvas of nature. i was a spectre of ryder; a raging maniac streaking like cheetah into the hysterical fire.

ii

the heavens were still and cold. my teeth were chattering and i was damp with sweat. it was breaking. i was ok. i spread the red skin over me and used the dough as a pillow. i had no need of memory. the stars were sockets; were militant dough-nuts. the field was dotted with land mines and loaves of bread. i broke one open. its guts were white, pulpy and pitted with deep purple seeds. hard insects shining and cracking under the pressure of my thumbnail. the cloud meat i ate. i filled and bloated and i rose. eventually i burst in/reign. the rain rendered the mines ineffective. i covered my head and ran in safety under a tree shaped like a teepee. out of habit i shook out my hair. it shocked me to find it gone.

in my pocket was a helmet of pink felt. i brushed it and hung it on a branch. the sun was shining. it was may day and in the distance the guardians of innocence were wrapping poles with satin streamers. i was reminded of the terror and beauty of a garden. the rose garden of my grandmother. the screen door was like the ocean. i was pressing my face against the mesh gazing across to afrika. ebony women were carving legs for tables. gleaming legs smeared with honey. i think it was honey because it was sticky. i felt fat and sick. i had eaten too much bread. i leaned against the side of a white framed house and puked. i had lost my dog tags. my shoes were gone and so was my money. over there, stuck, in the branches, was my head gear. i smoothed it out and put it on. i felt better. i was clean and shiny like the cheek of a lacquered apple. i was healthy. a fresh foot soldier. my sleeves and pantlegs rolled. my socks down. i looked beyond and another gleam revealed where i had been laying. i gathered my stuff and moved on.

are you an artist by any chance?

no

freelance?

no

no-no no-no no-no-no
no no-no no-no no no

i ran in indian rhythm. i ran for a long time with no fear nor destination. i just ran. like in/training. i was preparing for the marathon. i was a face in the newsprint breaking ribbon. suddenly i wasn't a rabbit anymore. i needed a goal. the runner returns to the stadium. i wasn't returning anywhere. one sharp moment of recognition. there was a splinter in my hand from the screen door. i had matches and a hem full of safety pins. i sterilized one and worked the splinter out. it was coated with gray enamel that refracted the sun.

this area was sparsely populated yet all the houses were identical. white framed houses with enamel roofing and siding. a girl is standing in the kitchen looking thru a screen. everytime her uncle takes her picture she squints. the sun reflects off the slick enamel and hits and shatters where she's been looking. i can barely make her out. for me getting my picture taken has always been uncomfortable. i feel too familiar with the camera; an eye that connects and freezes the present with one acoustic wink.

girl at bible school. girl in pleasure. girl standing in line at recess with an open face waiting to receive like sanction a big spoonful of raw honey. the sight of it made me sick. and i didn't like us all sucking off the same spoon. though we picked berries together i felt no sense of brotherhood. some of them i wouldn't even breathe with. sometimes i had to hold my breath in time with the exhaust on the bus. everything was returning, gushing and chattering out of synch like a home movie. soundtrack is the muffled voices of women. words projecting from the glazed faces of my ancestors. the green eyes of margarite and her madness. the slow, untimely death of a gentle woman. jessica, diaries and a harp.

music permeated the room like an odor like the essence of a flower. my sister was advancing; her mouth full of rose petals. is awareness evil? she was mischievious, wondrous. protected by an aura of innocence.

hours pass. where is my transistor? i'd like to hear the idiot. i like how the word idiot comes only once with a sonic beep punctuating it. the cut night clubbing. i imagine aliens moving in on a munich discotheque and injecting the air with jelly. a victim is chosen. a victim is one of the chosen people. a victim is stretched across the hump back of a volva and assaulted by parallel vocals—one frontal, one subliminal. the one in the background is the one you get your orders from. the one in the foreground is the utterer of orders. there you have the writer and the written.

i think i'll set up camp. repetition of a former formal formula. the money pillow, the long smoke and the book. the book takes the place of music. i have no idea where i am and no desire to ask. i am in munich and light is falling. i have a flash of inspiration. i dig a hole and line the soft earth with english pounds. i dump my stash and cover it over with the skin and leaves. i've stuffed several sheets with francs inside my shirt. i hail down a car and entertain the driver in exchange for a ride into town. I pay for an amp, an electric guitar, cords, picks and a strap. i promise to return in a few hours. i get me a hot plate, a weight of paper and a typewriter. in a remote section of town i find a room. it needs white washing so i offer pleasure to one of the local boys. he works as a waiter not far from this place in a rock n' roll club. he works for me but won't take anything in exchange. he brings me liquor and chewing gum and says maybe next time. he has no name and has the face of an angel.

the shops have closed. i can't pick up my purchases. i lie down on the single bed and look up at the ceiling. suddenly i feel dirty, agitated. if i were in rif, i would slip into my burnoose and barter with the night merchants. i grab a buttery jacket of chocolate leather and make my way down the dismal commercial streets. if this were somewhere else i should be returning with my arms loaded with oils and spices and bundles of mint. i walk for a long time. there is no one around. i am lost in the solar system of a modern german condominium. i hail a cab and have him drop me by the ramp of the club yes. i don't stay long because the women are giving me trouble. one gives me her necklace. one gives me everything. i take her in a car parked out in back. the music is loud and boring. the lights strobing. i was thinking of driving her back to my room but decided to take her right there in the car. i was grateful for her stupidity, her pretty dress and her quaaludes. i had her kneel for me. i had her bend and i had her nuts. i tweaked her nipples and numbed her pussy by massaging her with a low circular motion. she was still in panties. i worked her over slow and machine like. she lost control and dropped a shoe. inside it was a wad of german marks which i palmed. she opened for a kiss and i inserted a small pink eraser. i left her cursing and gagging and exited with my guardian angel on his motorcycle.

the essence of motorcycling is to be free. i have developed a taste for fear and since this taste i crave the drama of competition, the challenging dilemma of drugs and the dangerous glowing pit of communication called love.

i am not surprised we are going far away. far from my room far into the night. nothing surprises me. not his gestures, his silence, his coat nor our ride like an endless solo. a violent fuzz-tone. an organ coming on like orchestra. my lungs expand. i feel fine. my hairs grown in. i look like the dark side of a dutch boy. i feel happy i really feel great. i would like to be a guitar solo. one that resounds like bagpipes or bells. i would like to be the backside of a rickenbacker smashing against a limestone wall in replay on a raging newsreel.

IN ANOTHER DECADE ROCK AND ROLL WILL BE ART

we blew opium, brown bagged and reed piped. i knew exactly what he was going to do. he cradled my head then caressed and snapped my neck. i laid there unconscious but i knew what he was doing. every moment. he took the money and my wristwatch and the keys to my room. he kissed me all over. the stars were huge in the clear black sky. the fields were bright with starlight. i was trapped in the nocturnal landscape of an impossible soldier. i could feel his hands around my neck. and his fingers smoothing and manipulating the muscles that stretched over the bone of my collar. i exhaled as he pulled.

my lungs were full of water. it was raining. the stoic night rains of europe.

i was covered with mud. the grass had stained the cloth of my uniform. i walked for a long time in the rain until all traces of grass and sweat vanished. my wet translucent garments clung to my damp skin. dawn came with the sun. i was dry but i was unable to locate my original campsite. i hitched a ride back into town. i rode in the back of an open truck with four boys. each one gave me something. a mirror for signaling, a comb, a pair of brown shoes and a paper wallet. i braced myself against the panels as the oldest ripped the inner seams of my slacks. this way it was more like a skirt. they baste stitched the back and added a large red neckerchief to the front. all this action and i'm not moving. i was thinking of the night and what had happened. they were pinning my new skirt together, rolling down my socks and wrapping wild flowers around a crown of wire. all this movement directed toward my waist and head yet i remained motionless. i was gone. i was traveling.

i was rolling in the cornfield with my angel. the twist of wire slid down and encircled my neck. my tears caused it to rust then dissolve. the immediacy of this action scared the men. they yelled for the driver to stop and waved me off. i wandered aimlessly into the long drone of a velvet gown. the train seemed to go on forever. after a time i re-entered town still in rags. in the center of town there was a fountain. water streamed and increased. i knelt down into the stream where scores of tadpoles rush. the slimy algae twisted around my knee and down my calves jetting blue arteries over white clay. i washed my legs. there were scratches all over them. i picked some blossoms and fashioned myself a tiara of flowers. i looked at myself in the clear water. i had no opinion of my

face. i was bred for a higher system of vanity. i was exhausted.
i returned to my room.

the military blankets and the olive hopsacking on the win-
dows are gone. everything is fresh and sweet, bathed in the af-
ternoon light. there is a decanter of lead crystal on the sill. i
pour myself a thimble full of sherry, wash and retire naked on
the bed. i relive it all over and over.

i was a narrow waving tulip. i slept for several hours. when i
awoke he was standing there, watching over me. the amp was
there and the guitar was there. he grabbed my feet and we
started laughing and kissing. we were both very happy and
made love quickly. like a salutation. he fell asleep inside of
me. i eased out of bed. there was no reverb on the amp so i
washed my hair instead. it was down to my shoulders and the
color of copper. i cut it crusader style. i drew a thin blue line
connecting my eyes and a vertical line down my forehead thru
the center of my nose. i washed again then i washed his feet.
he was still and dreaming. i gathered his clothes in a bundle
with the exception of his blue coat. i could not imagine him
without it. i draped it over the wicker chair and brushed the
collar with the assured strokes of a chambermaid. he was ly-
ing there in a wrinkled shirt. the contours of his shirt crum-
pled like newspaper. adrenalin coursed thru me. a jagged rac-
er charged thru my veins. my fingers were sausages—shiny
and pulsing—full of crazy energy. the guitar felt good in my
hands. i didn't plug it in. i was racing with time and memory. i
imagined him standing beside me concentrating on disinte-
gration and bending notes. we were on the stage in a stadium
and the lights were low and mean. i was in a state of tempo-
rary surrender. song on the radio: bend for thee. i am bending
in half in service to him, for myself, for the moment and soon
everything is forgotten. memory is replaced with energy. i am

moving through a dense landscape lush and tropic. i am bending like a manic willow, like a finger in pain. only the moment and beyond the moment exist. sleeping he knows it and dead so he would also know it.

iii

his clothes i sacrificed. i salvaged nothing. i borrowed a small motor bike and rode out of town. pass the long shopping plazas. pass the spaced out beauties in purple half boots. pass the sex shops and the downtown club with its aluminum stage like the belly of a broiler. i rode for a long time trying not to conjure his face—his consuming face and his silence.

suddenly i was free. let it go i laughed and i did. i let it all go with a rush and a moan of truth. my next piece of luck was a landmark. a frame house with grey enamel siding. soon i was able to locate my belongings. everything intact but the muddied lining. i was happy to have retrieved my soft burden. i slung it over my shoulder and pushed the bike over on its side in the open field. existing within my consciousness and deeper—embedded in the realm of dreams and of fever—are our encounters past and future. as for the present he is always inside of me. as for future—perfect soon i would be stopping to have a rest and have a smoke.

everything eventually repeats itself. in the cool breath of dusk i already sense a point of boiling. perhaps there is a mutual lack of edge. i have a last smoke. tears not words pour. something is brewing, however vague. it is there lurking like a saint in the thick of the eucalyptus. deep and dense encounter with many little deaths. munich. it was not the first time i had left a guitar behind nor would it be the last.

high on rebellion

what i feel when i'm playing guitar is completely cold and crazy. like i don't owe nobody nothing and it's a test just to see how far i can relax into the cold wave of a note. when everything hits just right (just and right) the note of nobility can go on forever. i never tire of the solitary E and i trust my guitar and don't care about anything. sometimes i feel like i've broken through and i'm free and could dig into eternity riding the wave and realm of the E. sometimes it's useless. here i am struggling and filled with dread—afraid that i'll never squeeze enough graphite from my damaged cranium to inspire or asphyxiate any eyes grazing like hungry cows across the stage or page. inside i'm just crazy. inside i must continue. i see her, my stiff muse, jutting about in the forest like a broken speeding statue. the colonial year is dead and the greeks too are finished. the face of alexander remains not solely due to sculptor but through the power and magnetism and foresight of alexander.

the artist preserves himself. maintains his swagger. is intoxicated by ritual as well as result. look at me i'm laughing. i am lapping cocaine from the hard brown palm of the bouncer. i trust my guitar.

therefore we blackout together. therefore i would wade thru scum for him and scum is ahead but we just laugh. ascending through the hollow mountain i am peeking. we are kneeling we are laughing we are radiating at last. this rebellion is a gas which we pass.

ain't it strange

down in vineland/there's a clubhouse
girl in white dress/boy shoot white stuff
oh don't you know that anyone can join
and they come and call and they fall on the floor
don't you see when you're looking at me
that i'll never end/transcend transcend
ain't it strange/ain't it strange.

come and join me/i implore thee
i impure thee/come explore me
don't you know that anyone can come
and they come and they call
and they crawl on the floor
don't you see when you're looking at me
that i'll never end/transcend transcend
aint it strange/oh ain't it strange
true, true, who are you
who, who am i
oh da/oh da/oh da/oh da/oh da/oh da

down in vineland/there's a clubhouse
girl in white dress/boy shoot white stuff
oh don't you know that anyone can join
and they come and call and they fall on the floor
don't you see when you're looking at me
that i'll never end/transcend transcend
ain't it strange/oh ain't it strange

do you go to the temple tonight/oh no i don't think so
do you not go to the palace with me marie/oh no i don't
believe so no/see when they offer me book of gold
i know soon still that platinum's coming/and when

i look inside of your temple it looks just like the
inside of the brain of any one man and
when he beckons his finger to me well
i move in another direction/i move in another dimension

hand of god feel the finger/hand of god i start to whirl
hand of god i don't linger/don't get dizzy/do not fall now
turn whirl like a dervish/turn god make a move/turn lord
i don't get nervous oh i just move in another dimension

come move in another dimension
come move in another dimension

egypt

in the desert of wait ting/ting
nobody gets it
the essence the absolute filth
and treble
vines of existence
performance for all sects
layers of skin to pop
the syrupy dunes
the inside of a cheek
talk is formal
possessive
and base
lowest adult male
coarse tough fiber from palm
our hands are arthritic
fixed lost and held over
into the following chord
we scratch across the sands
scale the seizure
the immediate terrain
stretches of sandpaper
stroking perfect skin
i am silent and setting
w/ hands folding
before my flabby egyptian
pharoahs are very heavy
akin to one of the harvest
limbs of the in/chain
at peace w/ the solid fold
impossible not to worship
imparable as to damage
impartable as to message

scrawled on the surface
of the desert of waiting

confession i read thee
like the will of the quaran
see that you greet me w/ the sense
of a long stream of piss
i love and love the infinite
split and amoral heart
several chambers pumping
filled to capacity
like the ballroom of a masked hotel
the lovers withdraw
the lovers revolve
slow manikin profile
twisting skeleton positions
their eyes meet
there is no time for kisses
the sky is modest and sweet
as they excoriate passions
thru the profile of movement
love manifestoes en frescoe
the hacked enclosures
of blessed and incarnate rogues
skins of saints and rugs of prayer

the blue walls of the vase close in on me.
draw me into liquid shadows. lapis and limp
and cringing shadows suggesting nude entrances.
sadness projects a crystalline mass. a large wet
tear. a prosaic vessel housing a mind which has
gone omega.

there is a chalky rotation/white and tubular
there are years of returning/of knowledge

there is refuge in incest incense and past
there is burden and truth
in the shaved arteries of future

in the desert of wait ting/ting
no/one gets anything
i beg you to give me leave
do not bury me even as your kingdom
goes temple to journey
leave me no space
in your little boat
to pass from life to life and life
be content w/ this letter
and a handful of feathers
do not rescue me
i crave another destiny
the ghosts of our love
are drying
or dying
or worse.

rape

yum yum the stars are out. I'll never forget how you
smelled that night. like cheddar cheese melting under
fluorescent light. like a day old rainbow fish. what a
dish. gotta lick my lips. gotta dream i daydream.
thorozine brain cloud. rain rain comes coming down.

all over her. there she is on the hill. pale as a posy.
getting soaking wet. hope her petticoats shrink.
well little shepherd girl your gonna kingdom come.
looking so clean. the guardian of every little lamb.
well beep beep sheep i'm moving in.

I'm gonna peep in bo's bodice. lay down darling don't
be modest let me slip my hand in. ohhh thats soft thats
nice that's not used up. ohhh don't cry. wet whats wet?
oh that.heh heh.thats just the rain lambie pie don't squirm.let
me put my rubber on.I'm a wolf in a lambskin trojan.ohh yeah
that's hard that's good.now don't tighten up. open up be-bop.
lift that little butt up. ummm open wider be-bop. come on. no-
thing.can.stop me. now. ohhh ahhh. isn't that good.my.melan-
choly be-bop.

Oh don't cry. come on get up. lets dance in the grass
lets cut a rug lets jitterbug. roll those tiny white
stockings down. bobby sock-o lets flow. come on this is a
dance contest. under the stars, lets alice in the grass.
lets swing betty boop hoop
lets birdland lets stroll
lets rock lets roll
lets whalebone lets go
lets deodorize the night.

space monkey

blood on the tv/10 o'clock news
souls are invaded/heart in a groove
beating and beating/so out of time
what's the mad matter with the church chimes
here comes a stranger up on 9th avenue
leaning green towers/indiscreet view
over the cloud over the bridge /
sensitive muscle/sensitive ridge

pierre clemente snorting cocaine
the sexual streets it's all so insane
humans are running/lavender room
hovering liquid/move over moon

stranger comes up to him
hands him an old dusty polaroid
it starts crumbling in his hands
he cries ah man i don't get the picture
this is no picture this is no picture
this is just/this is just my jacknife

rude excavation/landing site
boy hesitating/penknife
he rips his leg open
he's so out of time
blood and light running
it's all like a dream
light of my life/he's dressed in flames
it's all so predestined/it's all such a game
for space monkey/so out of time time
for space monkey/so out of line line

space monkey/in a state of grace
and it's all just space/just space

there he is/up in a tree
oh i hear him calling down to me
that banana shaped object is no banana
it's a bright yellow ufo
and it's coming to get me/and here i go
up up up up up up up
oh goodbye momma/i'll never do dishes again
here i go from my body
ha ha ha ha ha ha
help!

suite

the black screen. the glittering lights of the river.
the boy in black uniform high on a hilltop with his
hair blazing. the boy raises his arm to nature.
nature, restless and moody, does the unspeakable—
she extends her hand. a siren a sound so disarming
he lets go and is ravaged by sharkless teeth, a
set of teeth afloat in the ribbed waters. nature,
in another time another period, caused them to be
extracted from her lover—the basking shark.

citizens! we must not sleep.
our sons are running like seasons to nature.
man the tower and trestle with tenderfoot soldiers.
daughters! be awake at the wake
be you rigid and immobile and in guard.
citizens! resurrect your sons from this sad spot of decay.

the woman the tree and the arms equal nature.
the cry is take me with you. rolling in beds of salt
within the agonizing dimension of stillness she is
coming. coming in his arms. coming in fiber.
i love you, whispers nature.
a ragged whisper like the threads of her gown.
a garment of water with the texture of dusting powder.
just as he would be kissed by death he is falling back.
he must pull away he needs his hand. his nose itches.
the granite lifts.
the angry swell of water charging into cloud
cloud is confused
clouds are rearranging
adjusting slate

silhouette of the boy and his mother
her hair is a mane of survival
her hair, plaited, is a weapon
she is the womb of return, the protractor
she extends her hand she ruffles his hair
she covers his head with a cap of black wool
the shock of iron the wailing of women
one night it will happen it will happen again
he is bound to step thru
humping the space
between death and death
the medieval trumpet
the clarion
the clarinet
a solo of holes
a boat of stardust
a laundress
notes bad and tender
and the claustral joining
encounter in space
the boy w/ the black river
as he turns in the arms of nature
who worships the flaming sons of women

III. SISTER MORPHINE

two masks
making love

notice 2

joke: once, if I remember well, I sat judy on my knees
        and...

how, when all else failed: bird, magician, desert mirage,
the prospect of gold and riches beyond the cloak and sleeve
of marco polo, I attached all to a woman.

caught like a squirrel on high tension wire. a woman worthy
of worship of monastery. with every vice divine. no morals
required etc. this love, at first glance, a concrete and very
fertile egg. later to be cracked and revealed as colossal
pride. as there and as fruitless as the parthenon
    (sans goddess).
the tourists postcard. the illusion of grandeur.

picking over the ruins of this romance this comedy like
        hungry
prehistoric. slender minarets, white and crumbling like sugar
teeth. song (this moment) on the radio: as I walk this land
of broken dreams.

blushing monument: pink sphinx. sizzling squirrel. fallen
pharoah. the exhaustion of the mind which attempts to
penetrate the mystery of her.

judith

some of many facemasks

judith. a jewel. some call judea judas judex
and finally me in my own affectionate manner:
ju ju bead. my little candy.

most likely one would suspect I was just
sweet on her. juicy. not so. I have it for
her from every angle. shes the icing on my
cake. angel food.

i love her like the jews love the land.
i love her like judas loved jesus.
oh dont be surprised. his mad love for our lord.
it makes one dizzy dizzy dizzy dizzy.
silver was mere glitter in the eye. it was the
kiss of death that was gold pure gold to him.
judas was the true diver. plunging into the
arms of gods fated son. illustrating the
drawbacks of homosexual love.

yet here i go gazing after a girl. ah spansule.
hollow pill. whats in it for me. perhaps the love
of judy. judy judy judy. punch punch punch.

i love her like judex (the free lance magician)
loved the maid. the perfect image of a girl.
kodak. the daughter of eve before she ate the
avocado.

yet green eyes golden haired she is not.
she is no angel baby. no candidate for a

glass slipper. she is not the kind of girl
youd find in an eyebrow pencil ad.
no jelly bitch.

but the girl I'd like to touch. we've shared
a bed but I could not touch her. she turned
on her side. I could not touch her. rustling
of new sheets. a very humid memory. but I
could not touch her. nor would she touch me.
plea plead pleading.

victims of the conceit that women were made for
men. radium. I turn out the light. I would not
touch her. after a while desire is overcome.
sooner or later desire hides behind the skin.
retracts. retreats. then sleeps and sleeps and
keeps on sleeping.

georgia o'keefe

great lady painter
what she do now
she goes out with a stick
and kills snakes

georgia o'keefe
all life still
cow skull
bull skull
no bull shit
pyrite pyrite
shes no fool
started out pretty
pretty pretty girl

georgia o'keefe
until she had her fill
painted desert
flower cactus
hawk and head mule
choral water color
red coral reef
been around forever
georgia o'keefe

great lady painter
what she do now
go and beat the desert
stir dust bowl
go and beat the desert
snake skin skull
go and beat the desert
all life still

a fire of unknown origin

you're displeased
maybe I should just stop
being you

A fire of unknown origin
took my baby away
a fire of unknown origin
took my baby away
swept her up and off
my wave length
swallowed her up like the ocean
in a fire thick and grey

death comes sweeping
thru the hallway
like a ladies dress
death comes riding
down the highway
in its sunday best

death comes driving
death comes creeping
death comes
I cant do nothing
death goes
there must be something
that remains
death it made me sick and crazy
cause that fire
it took my baby
away

she left me everything
she left me all her things

edie sedgewick
(1943–1971)

'i dont know how she did it. fire
she was shaking all over. it took
her hours to put her make-up on.
but she did it. even the false eye-
lashes. she ordered gin with triple
limes. then a limosine. everyone
knew she was the real heroine of
blonde on blonde.'

oh it isnt fair
oh it isnt fair
how her ermine hair
turned men around
she was white on white
so blonde on blonde
and her long long legs
how I used to beg
to dance with her
but I never had
a chance with her
oh it isnt fair
how her ermine hair
used to swing so nice
used to cut the air
how all the men
used to dance with her
I never got a chance with her
through I really asked her
down deep
where you do
really dream
in the mind

reading love
I'd get
inside
her move
and we'd
turn around
and turn the head
of everyone in town
her shaking shaking
glittering bones
second blonde child
after brian jones
oh it isnt fair
how I dreamed of her
and she slept
and she slept
and she slept
forever
and I'll never dance
with her no never
she broke down
like a baby
she suffocated
like a baby
like a baby girl
like a lady
with ermine hair
oh it isnt fair
and I'd like to see
her rise again
her white white bones
with baby brian jones
baby brian jones
like blushing
baby dolls

judith revisited (fragments)
the ladies room is ravaged

i.
your tribe. white car. a whole spectrum of whites. whiter than
the knight. her matinee pearls. the dress shirt of judex. the ma-
gicians glove. whiter still than the dove in the hand.

holy ghost? no baby this is no symbol this is for real. crystal-
lized vapor cold powder. snort that cerebral stuff. put your
tongue in my mouth. body and brain it spell cocaine. speed
and slow motion. inner search light. or have I been robbed?
jack-off in the bathroom. perfect snow job.

electric brain-o. hairy halo. itchy claroil. me I blonde now. ad-
mire mirror what is paler? linen napkin. coconut chiffon cur-
tain. the bridal bed. mother milk. wrinkled sheet. extraction of
teeth. immense ivory. bash my brains out. egyptian maggot

ii.
sudan the royal secret. mining and extraction guarded. ivory
cone. cone gun, mujah. juju extracting my teeth and bleach
tonsils. atom ideas alkimia blood love between us serve pur-
pose, allow me to relax as well as give her confidence, amateur
operation with handful of small tools. novocaine adminis-
tered with miniature hypodermic

iii.
only lips move. love poem call silk root. ruined roman/ anna
magnani/ rose over tokyo/ lick a cultured pearl I'm ancient
I'm stunning I'm just your style. your seed your private dilem-
ma. my dentist hogwash. theres spit on my teeth. aren't you
afraid they'll find out about us. how we hump it up in the out-

house. how you love my fist up your ass. do you burn my let-
ters confess. or are they locked in a closet in some roll top desk
medicine chest strong box poste box anywhere with a kee-ee.
no worry I'll sleuth them out every envelope. me I detective. a
very private dick. sniff sniff beagle brain. your bush needs
clipping. your mouth needs kissing. dog kiss. tu-lips. want
you so much my jaw ache. feel your rayon tit. in the open
mouth of your corvette.

honey feel so crazy. not stylishly. not brilliant. just so I cant
remember the last sentence. what I was looking for. the mo-
ment before. daydream has no plot characters just words.
strung together. no not loosely. you arent listening. tight
dense just like tom thumb rhino choker.
correction: pearl choker.

iv.
juju. what are you writing? a party invitation. only lips move.
my upper lip is frost bit. puffy a blonde ubangi. bite me a lit-
tle. bite me a lock of your hair. bite me a hot dog. no give me a
bite to eat. what you write?

you draw palm tree/i drink pepsi
i want to be a landscape painter.

oh thats good. thats very good. we go to red sea. you paint a
pyramid you paint your toes red. and me I stay in bed. I hold
my head. freeze all that is said. only words move.

v.
oh jesus write it out of your body patti. wait wait all night.
weary day. is snow too romantic? we could do it in the snow.
washing your hair. bending over the tub. running my soapy
forefinger down your spine. you on your knees bent over the

tub. your breasts out of shape swaying like two golden bells. i'm the gardener you're lady chatterly. i stand up. turn around and suck my dick.

washing your hair. maybe too romantic. so what clock. i imagine you on the nile. that neck of yours enough to make Nefertiti blush. the delicious white slump of your shoulder after lovemaking after

love it wears off. there's grass stains on your dress. we are nearly finished. a cold july with her. in her sunsuit. her fleshy legs. when I press my thumb against it makes a white mark. the powder on her wrist. how she never removes her heavy bracelets (african) even to make love. her ballet scar. all things pure.

human? no mam. go away from them. mistress is gelatin. atom.

she's a football player. one night. no its dusk. in back of the bleachers. blondest sweetest football virgin. hardon softest leather buttocks. lick it up her delicious teen-age sweat. show her how. make her again. leave her dazed confused exhausted defiled spidered black as coal. oooy-gooey all over her high school letter. kick her in the side. in the ear. words pour

i leave you laying there. i am intact. and i dont care.
(rimbaud)

marianne faithfull

*"i was born in hampstead. my mother wasnt
screaming so they didnt believe she was in
labor. later i went to convent school. later
i rode in leather. later i took some sleeping
pills. i needed to lose . . ."* m.f.

there is a sweetness
in your little girl mouth
and the pearls you hold
in the palm of your hand
everytime you extend that hand
you break down you fantasize
you are circumcized
agonized
scourged
crowned
crucified
pierced four times
your sacred heart bleeds
drips and drips down
women weep at your feet
twelve men turn you
twelve men desire you
(ammonia clouds your armpits)
a starfish quivers in your belly
and the arrows shake out
shake out shake out
and the muscles in your heart ache
a fish slaps back your face
you roll you roll over
in the sanctuary yards
in a coarse black dress
bless your hot virgin mouth
you would be judas
and christ himself
you would be Mary Magdalene
the only woman
who made our savior weep
yet you would pull mandrax in
like the sacred wafer

leave me for eternal sleep
I wont let you go. no.
but no. I wont let you go.
I wont let the honey drain
from your sweet sweet box
wont let the crowds blush and gasp
while you carry your cross
wont let the flower girls fan you
hind a big black hearse
wont let the pearls
crumble crumble
from your little girl mouth

sister morphine

contemplation, peace within the eyes of an animal. the pink light surrounding the cold structure of egg and minnow caging the cosmic guerilla.

the sensation of freezing, of slobbering the northern lights shoot through my feet, an embrace of heat, light and gas. payment-ice.

one must return and retain the power of concentration. in order to reclaim the known and savored system of discipline one must focus. where there is no energy there is carcass. pure waste. nothing exists, it's just a stretch of meat. the music on the radio sucks and is pulling me down through the carpet. i got to get up and put a record on but its so fucking hard to move. i do it. i like this record marianne faithfull. she sings sister marshall. once, a long time ago, i checked into the alton house with my friend, in pain. his nerve was exposed and he laid for several days on the bumpy rusting cot draining and weeping. from the room next to ours came the moans of a willow bending in rhythm to the watershed of my friend. one night, in desperation, i called on the voice. i had never seen him but i had slept on the fire escape breathing through the morning in term with his wailing, his tolling, his haunting songs of wind.

when he opened the door i dropped down. he took my hand and we started dancing along the expansive curve of a staircase. he was crooning undertones. his was the pursing aura of a harmonica, a transonic system of phrasing that rendered me selfless. a cell fish crossing thru the air currents; the thruways of the flesh. his voice was the tone of light entrapponed in the cool ruins of an echo chamber. he led me to the bed. we laid down. there i was the ear—the whisper seeker. his words were itchy wings brushing my palate. the seat of the sense of taste.

—i need
—i know
—my friend is in pain
—his pain is your pain

he is not moving but he is whirling. he is already riding the curve of the wind. he rips open my shirt. it's paper. my skirt he lifted and pressed his hard bone against my sex which, like my clothes, gives in to his touch. sliding like sun w/no sound. there i was his by the power of his desire. i peeled for him, layer after layer, like the labia-erectus of the artichoke. the surrounding components in the room loomed as potential obstacles. my ankle cracked against the turntable.

—i'm going to fuck you
—i'm afraid
—i know
he had inserted a finger. a hard seering tentacle
which hooked even as i had resisted a hook. moving
in form w/the steel muscles of a machine.

he withdrew. he returned w/a heavy satchel of folded cloth. he opened it on the bed. there were his works—a small greased spatula, metal implements for spreading, tubing, a sterilized incisor and a rubber syringe for injecting fluid.

—oh please don't
—i have to
he irrigated quickly. he shot me up in/sanction.
before he shot he prepared the canal w/a lubricant
composed of grease and dry ice.

—your pain is my pain
—let go, he commanded
—i can't
—i know
—i can't
—you will
lie still, he said. he gripped me hard.

his cock was a doberman piston.
his eyes were blank, animal
melody oozed from his pores.
he was free of the burden of language.
free to jam in the realm of sound.
—let go
—i can't
struggle to achieve that which you have sacrificed.
struggle to rip thru your barrier of silence
—i can't
sound
wallpaper
animal
ceremonial
nuptual
we know
we rend
we end

i return to my friend. he is sleeping. i pour into his ragged
breath. he inhales, he releases, he relaxes. i sponge him down
and cover him over. i boil some water, stuff the pot w/mint
and make myself a strong cup. i wish to retire, but i am dis-
tracted by fluttering images.

here is a photograph of faith in the shape of a little bird. here
is a very fragile granule. the record is still revolving. she has
been trembling vibrato all morning. the scream of the ambu-

lance. i imagined my friend dying. i flash blood all over the
place. the atmosphere is chaotic. warm and icy. i imagine i am
preparing my pipe. i imagine myself smoking while reclining
on the bed of ingres. i must get a piece of the high ice from
which vibrating lice swarm and rub it against the gums in my
neck. i must submit and observe and take notice . . .

the staff of the prophet is not to be guarded as treasure, but is
to be handled and worked like the divining rod. do not abuse
the life force of a staff left to lead by stationing it in the badly
lit corner of a museum.
ART NEEDS LIGHT
look at the lack of it. here is one condemned to
display her purity for an eternity from a pedastool
of spice and despair. the tears caused the color
of the cumin to run like jagged ochre fingers over
her pouting body.
—there's a message here for you in my belly
—i know
—the message is infinite space, telegraph
—i know. i feel you.

only by dwelling in the pit can you create
to be delivered is to be raised.
the creator is delivered
determined he rises
thus it is that pain gives man wings
adroit maneuvers
shoulder muscles pulled gently
from the glassy blades
i cut my finger on the window
the panes are broken
there is no one on the street
my arches hurt i want out i'm afraid
the high dog rips one to shreds

fear, regret mere axis in the blend. i tried to resist but it was
the burning. his pain was my own so i reentered his room. he
was looking thru the window. he shaded his eyes from the
glaring sun. his guitar raced thru space like a violin because of
the graced violence in which he handled the neck. the frets
rose like the hips of women. their hot concaves straining to
merge with his fingerprints. to abuse and shock his sanded
tips.

between the bookends she was being crushed like a used stat-
ue. i helped her down and combed her hair. the last virgin, we
dressed her in a coverlet of ecru lace the color of a saw wood
shelf. i watched him trace the outline of her breasts. she was
wearing a baby blue wireless bra. desire itself caused her nip-
ples to erect little tributary temples of lust.

i knelt down and prepared the solution. i looked up and he
had entered. she was a vascular mass of shudders and sweat.
relief was rushing from her swelling heart. something burst
inside of her. it was the tongue of a chinese dog lapping and
twitching
like a shoulder. she was winking and stretching.
he moved over toward me. we circled like two pit dogs.
sometimes she can help me forget what a bitch you are.
an animal that never relaxes.
the room was littered with cigarettes and bottles
and polaroid packs.
—this is my last shot of you
—this is my last shot at you
—this is your last chance to come thru animal.
behind my heart there is a key floating
in a tank of dry ice there is spare vapor
in a mold i am shaping equations
twisting muscles

reckless maneuvers
baby i can't reach you
baby can't i reach you?
is there no one who can reach thru?
he fell back and he whined
in the midst of this cry i cried out
if he heard it he didn't recognize it
yet she retrieved it
like a dog
like a faithful dog
filled with eyes and space and peace
hail my lady full of grace
and waste and gas
tremulous and sad
deer face
sleepy whore
you yawn
and we score
we rend
we end
the 5x5
landslide
we snowball
we die
tear after tear
the excretion of sorrow
let me piss in your face
face fauna incarnate
we have shot up together
we shall do it tomorrow
adiós
sister morphine
sister morphine
mañana

IV. PIPE DREAMS

bread

near rosetta, there is the sepulchre for the arabian saint of slaughter. this erection was made by a woman whose name is not remembered. only the image of the name remains. the desert rose. a stone with all the color and attributes of the perfumed flower. she gathered these wonders from the long expanse of the surrounding deserts and with these she caused the foundation to be built.

for a long time she suspended the construction of the house and monolith so as to inspect what had already been made. when the moon was full she'd venture down alone and make it her place to lie down on the fitting of stones that was to be the slab for the intense sleep of the saint. a bed of roses. nature herself had etched the mulled impression of petals into a compote of sand and sawdust.

every night bathed in light and even as the moon phased out she would return to her stony sleep. her sleep became one with the bed on which she was sleeping. after awhile she was a stench. then a dream. the body of slaughter was not discovered. an unknown architect completed the work by the word of her word, making only one comment on the work—a rose carved in the summit and no covering for it. there moonlight was able to pass through and onto the slab on which she had been sleeping.

as there was nobody laid to wake there was no one who would believe this place to be one of sanction and grace. they took the woman to be a djnn, a disgrace. but because of the powerful presence of the architect no one dared to deface the sepulchre. a structure of wavy ordinance; at once modest and imposing.

each night the architect entered it and lay down and gazed up through the lovely hole and thought of the life he had spent in action. His attachment to dreams, memory and attainment. he had informed her of his impending torture.he had led her on a path of preparation for the continuum. one of understanding and of mutual practice.

they had agreed to meet in the garden the night it happened. he was leaving an adjacent quarter when suddenly he was surrounded by seven men. all closing in on him. club the saint they said and they were ready. their cause was his cause. death, martyrdom and resurrection. club the saint they said and they did. he lay there in the alley for several days and rotted away and days later was revived thru flesh from the bed of roses.

there his flesh was her flesh and he was alive and shining. his carcass was the curious scent of mint and flesh drifting within the hard petals of dust.

he lay there all through the night. a victim of tender slaughter and the wages of moonlight. he was condemned to live without her. she had lain in the same place, her tongue flashing as she imagined his kisses. as he, her caresses.

night and day and night and day. the arabs passed the sepulchre of slaughter. they caused their women to cover their faces. where there is no love, they said, there is no body. within was the architect. he was lying there passing through the leaves of their lives and their love which was wide and glowing and nourishing like chosen loaves of bread.

sterling forest

young huo-chiv the wonderful archer is introduced by his sister to the emperor han. soon he rises as the greatest warrior on horseback. slaying the enemy pushing back the huns. one totally miraculous, untouchable. a blonde mongol scourge and ruin to those against han and to the people of han - the chosen one. he merged with a christian. one radiant, silent, and on the eve of his greatest battle, very pregnant. on the field victory. in the chamber a fat baby girl. young huo-chiv returns. it is his 24th birthday. he kisses his wife and child. then the archer lies down on the bed alone and expires, like raymond rousselle, his face turned to the door.

grass

the sheet—cold and white and mystical along the grass—it
beckoned them. they endure. they explore all the regions of
their separate terrains and project with mutual pleasure the
rhythums of an ecstatic voyage. to resolve the riddle of bone
to bone.

a gang (japanese terrorists) attack the girl. terrified, she sub-
mits. the ineffectual juttings of angry arms—her bird shoul-
ders tremble. she is amazed by the fruitful energy of the
clouds. kimonos flapping. wings of furious lords flocking to
the territory. will they never cease fucking her? two nail her
ankles. one grips her hips. a blue haired warrior claws and
sucks her breast. thick stalks creme and pump. everything
opens and falls, clashing like obsolete armor. will she never
cease ascending?

the teeth of the boy gleam and bead. tiny stars studded with
ruby only inches from his face.and only a few feet away,
beyond the pleasure crypt of the girl, lies the sheet, white and
mystical, in the grass of their precious youth.

vandal
(happy tears)

he had done it! he had captured the storm
in a glass box. happy tears slid from his
eyes onto the box and down his wrist into
his cuff and slit of his elbow. tears were
streaking the glass with bars of shadow. all
around him there was silence. an empty
squad car. the closed and accusing eye of a
passerby. the terror of a little girl in a yel-
low raincoat. the anguish of the parched
streets. the freaked and brittle bones of the
laborers. the abusive gestures of the farm-
ers and the women w/split and starched
hairs. in the mirrors, wrath in myriad.
death and destruction duplicating and his
smile reflecting from the glass box where
he held the storm as captive after so long a
pursuit.

108

the amazing tale of skunkdog

don't be surprised if death
comes from within...

seven days and six nights the hero watched relentlessly.
horizontally under the sky. without food, drink or friend.
what was he after. what was he looking for.
a sign? an answer? a way out? something new.

now on the seventh evening of the seventh day hero
was holding on by a thread. lack of sleep, provisions
and loving arms was taking its toll. he ceased to
look up.

fair hero. he who was so intent on keeping his eyes
peeled immediately missed out.

for hero had made the sky jumpy. his piercing stares
put it on edge. when he finally looked down the stars
went haywire. cassiopia rocked like a cradle.

any chance observer unable to sleep. dreaming out
a window. counting sheep. would not have believed
his eyes. the milky way shook out shook out. a flock
of shooting stars. random comets. and the great dog
star so there like a new born moon.
yet hero saw nothing.

see a watched sky is like a watched pot. the minute
hero gave up the heavens boiled over. meteorites and
planet action passed over him like any common bat.
what could he say. he was in a mean condition. his

tongue was getting fuzzy to say nothing of his vision.
his eyes were seeing double of nothing.

was all lost? not on his life. it looked bad. but see
it this way: hero was finally getting down to earth.

suddenly (as in any monumental movie) there occured
a chain of events that pierced his very being; his
very soul. bursting his structure. giving all formal
experience the old heave-ho:
seven red ants bit his left hand
six smooth stones rolled from his tongue
his five fingers stretched an octave
four yellow feathers appeared from nowhere
as did three blue birds
over his head (halo) circled two luna moths
he was hungry so he snapped like the iguana
two moths were eaten.
his stomach fluttered
he was numb black out
sleep overcame him
(for one minute only
tho it seemed like hours)
and he dreamed this dream:

HOPE HE IS IN NO DANGER

he is led to the spawning ground of certain
sacred animals. he fears he will be forced to
copulate with one. native dancers circle him
then close in. they strip him down. his birthday
suit has changed clothes. he has a new feminine
figure. they cleanse him. they polish his body

with ox-blood oil. he is instructed to choose an
animal.

a striped tom brushes his leg. a grey and gold
tom with big blue eyes. eyes so blue heroes mouth
waters. a slick skinned cow with lacquer red udders
(very chinese) stretches and rolls in a mound
of cornflowers. blue flowers. bluer than the
cats eye.

hero wonders about his own eyes. in this atmosphere
do they also appear bluer than they really are?
damn not a mirror in sight. will the effect wear
off when he returns home? he hopes not.

to his left are the green green hills. a cold
menthol green. he glances over and gasps.
he sees skunkdog.
it is a huge mastiff with long shining hair. black hair.
his joint, unlike most dogs with their slimy rouge
pistols, is pure white. hero throbs down there like
a woman and cannot resist making an obscene gesture.

skunkdog opens his eyes wide. two huge blue saucers.
the bluest eyes imaginable. bluer than the cornflowers.
bluer than the mediterranean sea.

hero is overcome. wanton. he turns away then looks back.
oh no! skunkdog is gone. hero races across to the
green hills. he is naked and children are laughing.
he could care less. he uproots trees, plants and
boulders. he pulls his hair out by the roots. everywhere
strange animals are mating. steam is rising. women are

eating whale meat. other women are exposing their
bellies.

down a gully he spies skunkdog. he's been skinned.
there is his fresh carcass. hero falls prostrate.
gets set to grieve. when, out of the blue, he is brought
the skin of his slain beloved.
he slips it on.
its a perfect fit.
he is no longer hero.
he is no long hero
but black haired blue eyed

SKUNK DOG!

doggod dog/god doggod
the dog jumps over the moon.

konya the shepherd
(*for lenny kaye*)

this is the story of konya the shepherd. the land was parched and dry and the throats of the women were dry and folding. the sheep had long since been slaughtered and no lamb had escaped ritual. none, that is, save shamsa the black. the people had given up the will to dream their desire for prayer and even the need for visitation. only the arched necks of scourged believers, the pop eyes of the lookout station and the ancient holy men in suspension remained. relics. that was all.

but the radiant rhythum of change...potential change...the reign of words that whetted the palates and plates of man...the charge of light that electrified sky and eye...days and nights that made the earth moist and caressed the mouths of flowers ...dew on the lips of creation...the expectant pouts of wet and static children...all were going...literally gone.

there was nothing. nothing save konya the shepherd. resting his head against a stone and gazing at the crisp dry sky. black and white—a spray of diamonds on a sheet of carbon. sometimes the soft dust would cover him and he'd awake covered over with layers of black mist. travelers who passed would laugh and say that he had been kissed by shamsa the black. shamsa—the only survivor of the great flood of prayers that induced the great myth and the bloodbath of the lamb.

the bells tolled and the world turned. he was no longer the shepherd. he was konya the amateur astronomer—the watcher. the guardian of night. he had been kissed by shamsa the black and so he was kissing the sky. night after night. star upon star. night of planetary harmonics. night of perpetual change. each night each night. soon the night was wet with kisses. soon there was a storm brewing and the rain was also soon in coming.

there things were springing. the flock. the songs of women and the prayers. they sang not of the bad season but of kon-ya—the sky kisser—the spook sheep. soon the harvests would come. they soon would be threshing and weaving the prayer mats. soon the lambs would be fat and the stones of ritual cut.

the bells tolled and the world turned. konya the boy aimed arrows into the sun. konya the boy shot arrows into the profile of a butterfly poised on the nose of a stalk.

sandayu the separate

gravity eyes. eyes rimmed in kohl. girl resembles a young squirrel with slender rose arms. her skin is peach fabric. her eyes narrow and slant like geisha focusing pagoda stretched with net. buds jut the loose weave and cause her to be fixed in a swift tomb of blossoms.

the young prostitute suffers the rite of one thousand flowers. each blossom is gently pressed then slid into her sex until her womb and bowels are filled and blooming like the garden of sandayu the separate. bees and tengu sting and sweat honey. thorns, as sharp as steel points, are gathered from herds of roses. one such caltrop is highly polished. the girl is wrapped in gauze and escorted to the bathes of the master. here she is cleansed and scented with the oily petals of opiaha and jasmine.

sandayu enters. he bends down and carves an eye in the smooth forehead of his smiling wife. hand in hand they walk through the garden. the eye blinks, then focuses on the face of her husband. sweet light of nostrils he is seen at last! thus found he laughs and shakes the sky. he is no longer sandayu the separate but momochi, carver of the third new eye.

conté

there was a sultan who wanted a son. he had many wives but his magicians were clever—"no heir will seize our power," they pledged. each time a son was born he was slain and a girl child slid in place. this went on and on. daughters of unspeakable beauty ran barefoot thru the palace. after a time the sultan grew suspicious. he knocked up his new wife but good then decreed that he and his daughters would be present at the birth. the magician panicked but got a grip quick. they bribed the wife, the midwife and the daughters. a false birth was arranged. fatima groaned and quaked. the girl child was "pulled" and presented to the king. "another girl! praise allah! it is written that i, a king must harbor a chest full of women." at that moment true labor claimed his wife. "aieyee; the true child comes!" the king understood the magicians had tricked him. all looked in horror as the babe came.

"if it's a girl you'll be spared."

a tiny girl with green eyes erupted as the magicians regarded the king beneath crafty lids. yet even as they rubbed their hands—another babe! a son slid through the honey legs of the treacherous fatima.

the king slaughtered the women, the magicians, his wife and her daughter, took up his son and walked solemnly to the temple.

saba the bird
(revenge)

Sheba gave birth to six sons and then a daughter-saba, the
bird. it was written that saba be perfect and she was indeed
the pride of destiny. nothing however was said of the sons.
they arrived green and fragile; synthetic emeralds. the ruby
that was the mouth of sheba protruded from their tongues like
jewel-warts.

sheba adored her little frogs and attended to them personally.
she discovered they had all the maskings of an obscure tho
majestic choir. the music that erupted from their fused palates
was a banquet of sweet and fragrant melodies. high and disso-
nant chords. feverish modal structures. exotic and glorious
hymns.

she would lie back in a ring of breath and let their songs guide
the construction of her empire. they composed the tribunal of
ancient and forgotten sounds. they resonated the cherished
sins of apollo-the living lyre. thru the power of music they
sent sheba to the core of the earth. beneath the scared moun-
tains of kenya, not far from the baths of chosen women. there
was no delight that delighted her more than her transports
thru the love and language of her sons. the high priests, who
scorned the princes and resented her pleasures, looked to the
written.one to be their paladin.

in the moments she was giving birth to saba, sheba had in
mind to enter her daughter in song. the six were summoned,
but as saba came, head and limb, so were her brothers slain.
only one, tilag of charm, escaped. sheba passed off in grief

and was buried in grace by this surviving son disguised as a cultivator of the sacred grounds.

the high priests put saba under wraps. they were aware she was armed w/power but were unable to discover the source of it. seven years then seven more passed and they were still probing. all systems of sorcery, all secrets of alchemy and matters of code were spoken to her in tongue and riddle. they had hoped to trigger something locked deep within her so they revealed all to her yet she told them nothing. nothing was delivered and nothing suspect was demanded. she was content to lie about in the chamber of her mother, on pillows of cloud, draining the spheres of their music, drop by drop.

here was true dilemma. the priests had been prepared, thru the oracle, for one of miraculous charge. instead they were confronted with an indulgent child of unspeakable sensuality and beauty. angered and shaken, they left her to her pleasure and sought to consult the stars for a more fitting prophesy.

the miracle of saba was saba herself. she was a wave of silk, a cinema of movement. her glance made wet the optic nerve. she was no cool and secular moon like her mother. no sacred vessel sealed.she was hot, impulsive and open like the zipper of one who ravishes. she was a fresh and episodic monkey.

the power of beauty is underestimated. after a time she called the priests to her, one by one. she laid in her pillows of swan and opened her knees. frankincense burned and hung heavy and mystical over her bedding. one by one the senses of the priests were ignited. the fumes tangled with the hairs of their nostrils. two glow worms slid lazily, like tears, down her face and throat then dipped brazenly into the perfumed hollow of her collarbone. one by one the mediatory agents bent before her and kissed where the furry glows were kissing and sucked where they sucked.

the hand of saba was a blonde tarantula waltzing and teasing thru the folds of her dress—a breathtaking garment composed of layers of gauze and the lustrous fibers of indian corn. a costume washed in climbing jasmine, jeweled with the glittering humps of rare and milky insect larvae and loosely bound around her undulating body with the hamstrings of leopards.

the pale spider undid her. she was naked and calling to the guardian above her. soon each one sank and entered within her. the rude slayers of her brothers were lost and groaning in her temple.her eyes were wet and glad and full of triumph. she allowed them to experience the ectasy of her father then caused them to fall back from her shorn and defiled.

they laid away and trembled, still under her spell. they had failed to decipher the meaning of power that stalked, like a rabid animal, behind her uncontrollable beauty.her motive was gratification. her integrity-revenge. her treasure was the absolute beam of concentration. it allowed her to entrappon any living thing around her. thru the debasement of her guardians—the slayers, she was able to extract sensual vengeance; to relieve herself from the pain of desire and the burden of her mothers' unrest. a dual satisfaction that caused her to ascend and to desire higher.

the priests, no longer virgin, were spat on and defrocked. disrobed and ashamed they were condemned to crawl and become akin to all who would enter their temple. for saba had made public the massive edifice, wherein they had exercised the mysteries of night. they were now mocked and humped by the most wretched rapists and laborers and yellow strangers.

saba caused a wall to be built dividing her bed chamber and the new quarters of the scorned enemies of her brothers. impossible to penetrate transparent and smooth as glass, a missive was then sent thruout the kingdom. every face that had been sinned against was summoned before her. they were her delight and with them she would drink and dance and copulate. no/one was too grotesque nor too realized. she opened her ivory flanks to the greedy lapping tongues of christian women. she specialized in lepers and holy men. their assaults produced extreme unction. yet still she seemed searching for something for someone or a particular sensation which had no name.

in the anti-chamber the shorn ones were weeping and jacking. after a time they took to clawing their skin and ramming in/passion into the hard celluloid shield. saba had reduced them to glowing and wriggling worms—breast suckers, by infecting them with the high and mighty lust of solomon.

they had failed to convert, into intelligible form, the prophesy of a coming master via saba the bird. they had not seen that which was written in a name. she was the bird of paradise, the manifestation of the spirit. the ghost in flesh. all this they failed to see thru the blinding light of greed and self interest. they had failed to hear the song that drifted and so they would crawl and not be lifted.

everyone is talking/about the bird
do the bird bird bird
the birds the word

apres saba. after the sabbath. it was the hour of the tiller. she
was bathing with the leper when he entered. first she was
washed out and penetrated with a stick. between his teeth was
not a worm but a jewel. red and vibrant as the lips of sheba.he
mounted and pierced the hard seams of her true mission. she
was no longer virgin. the tears and blood of sheba and her
sons were rushing. saba was rising above and beyond the
point of wisdom and tension for which she was aiming.

she is saba the bird
the avenging angel
composed of 22 properties
11 saintly
11satanic
would cover and wing
even as the angel covers
yet defiles the door of a mosque
w/ her flying birdshit

merde. god. victory is hers. she is with seed. the accursed peo-
ple are her people. their spinning laughter her laughter. their
tears are her spasms, her magical moans. she is going beyond
her minds make-up. she is giving birth to her power in the
chamber of her mother. the sire is tilag whose voice is an essay
in celestial harmonies.

the child is balthazar—the donkey face
who will lead the people
thru the star saba is becoming
to the shining face of the savior.

thermos
(radiant coins)

love was in a constant state of liquid grace. love was the warm
and waxy elixir transported in the cool mercurial regions of a
thermos. thru the stark shadows she would crawl, the thermos
between her knees. the edges of her pantaloons hot and bil-
lowing. there were smooth golden tears embedded in the flesh
of her thighs. glowing stains of other such vigils. she d shim-
my from the sleep of harem into the austere recesses of the
Rea désheēd military barracks. sometimes the boiling coffee
would overflow and shock the silk of her cloth and waist. still
she'd go on until the thick and unmeasurable warmth would
reach the lips and throat of her one most beloved.

one night she was taken for a deserter and shot. the load
dropped from her shy trappings and hit rock. she was able to
retrieve it and make her way to the penile chamber—his pris-
on. she felt free only when she was with him, so she chose to
drop there in total submission before him. in the center of his
grief there was her offering. as always he unscrewed the lid
and took a long draught. uncertain of anything. save the end,
he was unable to decipher the code in agony of the gesture of
her right hand. nor was he able to comprehend the twitching
of his lids and hips. nor any spasm at all as the liquor and li-
quid glass cracked, chipped and made its slow slivery silvery
way through his bloodstream.

enculé
(cocksucker)

he is rising on a cycle. behind him is grain, woman and ma-
chine gun. he realizes she is calling for him, gasping and
straining in the privacy of her own nightmare. he could care
less. he has cut her off. this system of communication—energy
and telepathy only truly works when two are in tune. elsewise
it is mere yet pure voodoo.

he does not understand her commitment to obsession. he is
riding his motorcycle. she is miles away a long way away. she
has filled her neck and shoulders with him. she exhales his
name. she rests her head in the crux of her arm and imagines
his face and nuts full of light. he is alone and free riding his
motorcycle. he has cut her off so other forces are necessary.
soon he must stop. he rests his bike against a monument,
walks out into the field and shoots his load into the waving
grain. he believes he is alone but far away she has relaxed. a
servant enters and wipes the layers of glistening sweat from
her body. let go, she is told, and she has. she has exhaled his
seed into the valley of tears and is up again, on again, rising
on a cycle.

V. MOHAMMEDIA

the sheep lady from algiers

nodding tho the lamps lit low
nodding for passers underground
to and fro she's darning and
the yarn is weeping red and pale
marking the train stops from algiers.

sleeping tho the eyes are pale
hums in rhythum w/a bonnet on
lullaby a broken song
the sifting-cloth is bleeding red
weeping yarn from algiers

lullaby tho baby's gone
the cradle rocks a barren song
she's rocking w/her ribbons on
she's rocking yarn and needles oh
it's long coming from algiers.

pencillin

(living gods)

i have been lying here for a long time in stillness. it is dark,
complete. a room full of steamy warmth. around the bed is
comic debris—glowing, metallic. within i am dense cold
press. sick, immobile. i can't get a grip or feel. am i lead or
cloud? gravity is mysterious, ambivalent. milk ebbs thru my
veins—sluggish and rich. salamanders dip and move forward.

there is no wind. i have a police whistle in place of throne
(scream). i am unable to speak or sing. how sad everything is.
the glands in my throat are throbbing eggs. sinking into a
fresh pillow is a miraculous pleasure. i bless my bedding.

the physician entered, cool and needy. he gave me medicine
of health, mold of trust, because he did not understand i was
suffering from a malady of the spirit.

i loved him but i could not go w/him. we were condemned al-
ways to meet, to collide. my love filled him w/revenge. i had
nothing of his in my possession, no photograph or cloth. noth-
ing, not even memory. lying here my precious objects include
a white handkerchief and a vial of maroon and grey capsules.
the handkerchief is the barest egyptian cotton. a gift from a
woman, a corsican. it has served as a wrapper for a broken an-
gel. the angel i set w/my books. on the wall is a vellum sheet
from the ivory coast. this morning it slipped from the wall and
the angel—shot w/antibodies—took on the aura of skim.
someone joked that cortisone injections would build tissue
and eventually regenerate the arm.

my bed was filled w/hands. i never know what tense we exist in. as the penicillin moves like sluggish fish through my system there is also him. the knowledge and sense of him who i adore. in this time where allah does not speak and where communing in tongue w/god can only result in death, i prefer the company and crave the existence of living gods. i examine the angel, roll it around my palm and smooth my finger against its parts. the image of a plate, marked charity, reels through the room into an amplifier and smashes. the floor is littered w/the bones of china. one of these pieces resembles an arm. i need a razor. my dress is damp w/mist and sweat.

when i got up i cut my feet. there was blood everywhere but i felt nothing. i needed a razor to slice through the atmosphere. i groped around through the fog, shut my eyes and ran my fingers up and down the arm of my angel. i felt the calloused hands and fell to my knees and kissed them a million times. he desires surrender, i surrender. i give him. his hands cradle and readjust my skull. i am crying but i am not happy. perhaps someone will cover my head w/the handkerchief. then properly adorned i can be led to the front lines of the procession to collide within the realm of an imagined accident.

robert bresson

i

i awoke w/new strength.
les enfants terribles was on the screen. since my illness i have
installed in my sight a small screen and projection booth.
there are three films running continuously—terrible children,
mademoiselle and thomas the imposter. all blonde films. for
awhile there was only one film—au hazard balthazar. i saw it
several hundred times under mild sedation. for a time my
mind was a notebook of stills, annotations and the art of this
century.

specific, black and white. the enamel on canvas of pollock. we
are all children of jackson pollock. we are all chaotic mutants
—an extension of his action. from his mad wrist spun us. just
as we manifested our own assault upon hymn via the vocal
chords and kind of little richard and james brown or mick jag-
ger. just as we cheated within dance, a discipline of ritual
abandon. just as we thrust on our own and became one w/an
arm going down on the sonic set-up of an electric guitar. i
dream a lot of brancusi when i play guitar. his struggle w/mar-
ble is my drama w/rock. i like the feel of the neck. a strong sol-
id maple neck like the arm of a thick veined boy or the throat
of a conqueror.

ii

there is a close-up of marie. this is the same marie of one-plus-
one. the virgin guerilla gazes downward. like the siennese ma-
donnas she is able to hold a conversation w/the vein in her
neck. she is the artists model—eve the maniputable. she is the
victim—the sacrificial lamb of inspiration.

gerards hand is on her neck. his hands, like his clothes, are covered w/ the extract of action-oil. like the artist he is what he does. his clothes are black because he is a poet. black is the uniform, the skin of poets. his clothes are black and so is oil— his medium. w/it he can abstract language into the physical hieroglyphics of convergence, of blue poles. art is work. work is a conscious act. art is a conscious act requiring the harnessing of the subconscious, nuclear energy and the discipline of the spirit. to create and to also create distance. then there is the inventor—the miracle of the telephone wire—the power corridors of detroit. where there is electric power there is violence. electric violence is man at his highest. marie is in the process of birth. gerard is swallowing lugers shaped like candies.

gerard equates painting w/ a car skidding, crashing and sputtering. like no: 11, 14 this is no accident. the final icon is blue-printed behind his eyes. he knows what he wants to see and controls destruction. he pours oil over the road. he waits in the open field, his hands on his hips, laughing. one boy blends into another. his motorcycle, displaying the colors of maries tattered dress, lies on its side. he waits. he wants to feel what it tastes like to view the destruction of his creation in the process of ultimate completion. his expectations (fire, murder) are limitless. he harbors no potential remorse. he is a monster no less considerate than his brothers:

—de-kooning: decomposer of women
—gorky: illuminated coward
—rothko: black truth
—pollock: licensed killer

he also desires to witness his own immediate reaction to his creation and gradually the reaction of others. the reaction of the woman discovering her bleeding husband is a work of art. gerard is the creator but there are subcreators. a photographer raises his pentax and shoots her face. one shot follows another. the first shot was magic, a stolen moment. fresh grief is snowballed by test shots...into tri-x carcasse of sorrow.

the daughter wanders senseless into the field. the boy pulls her down w/him and forces her knees open. she is unable to speak or cry out. she is on the verge of phasing totally. he fucks her into awareness. when he feels the cry, gurgling and making its way up her throat, he silences it by jamming the chain from his bike between her teeth. now he is going to fuck her slow. he is going to witness her submission while her father is dying. as she spasms, her hand clutches the grass and clover. the hand of her father slips and ceases its grip. here is another great work. her will and action are acting independently. here she is a criminal. a victim gives in; she is a participant. she is actively participating in her own glorious rape and the pathetic silent death of her father. she is no longer innocent but a living breathing work of art.

gerard is at work. all these details, his merging with woman, his destruction of man and nature, all are necessary components. the parts which will make up a total picture and the only true portrait of jackson pollock—coward, murderer and slob. a master pissing on the arched curls of villon. a master monster whose work resembled an arranged composite of the days and nights of bungling. a frenchman is the first to recognize him. jackson pollock—the first true american artist wrestling with a totally american dilemma.

his death and his blood and the blood of bunny was his finest work. it spattered and shot like the first breath of a gusher. gerard thinks of these things as he is being shackled. he is being led to prison. his gesture says no. if a criminal is a failed artist then he is no criminal. look around. the girl, limp and gone, kisses his feet. over there, in the road, the door of the car merges permanently with the face of the deceased. the red light circles the weeping woman. the highway is littered with flash cubes and greasy debris. this is my finest work he tells them. i did this with my eyes open and my conscience naked and light. the man with the pentax will receive an award from the press for the woman's scream. what will i receive and why do you crucify me?

they chain him to a tree. he rubs his chin against the bark. then his cheek and mouth. he opens his lips and shoots his tongue in-and-out, hard-and-fast like a jet of healing seltzer. he presses against the tree. he is thinking of the girl and her violet neck. he is spurting in his pants, through his pants, onto the tree, into the limbs of life right there at the scene of action while they question him.

there is oil on the road.
this oil is the cause of the car going out of control.
what we want to find out is who put the oil there
and what the motive was.
• who put the oil there?

i did.
motive
art.

i had to recreate the death of jackson pollock
w/the same radical destiny that spun from the
hallowed designs of his own death.
image: no. 11, 14 and portrait of a dream
image: the woman, lee krasner, shading her eyes
with hands brown and spotted.
here we have no accident no crime but a lateral
translation of a man going out of control
the initiation of a girl
(the intimacy of model and clone)
who would teach
as her teacher
taught her.
axle grease
film of sorrow
who put this oil here?
i did.
motive
art.
who was your teacher?
robert bresson

carnival!
carnival!

carnival! girl in black dress w/white cuffs advances. beads of youth gather on her peach flesh. 36 movements become 36 perfect stills from the same movie. cinema is so exciting, murmur the spectators, caressing their parts. we are the feminine corridors. the hallway of pink gloss. we are the taut lights and the forequarters of a bull. tourists jack-off as the movie keeps moving and carving credentials on the storage bin of stars.

the door opens. a crack. the girl w/cracked lips silently opens her knees on the bed of avengeance. the man w/coarse hands. the glistening sheets of ice pressed to her face. the melting floats. colorful ribbons and flags dragged thru the soggy rink. cold ghost of the girl advancing.

walls. pink slabs. no door knob nor the promise of a hidden spring. faces no features. faces bound w/wet gauze...

i awoke to radio rendezvous. transistor screamers. porno reggae. it was independence day. white boys without shirts gathered in/tense circles across the street. spanish girls in white dresses danced on the hot paving. an athletic yellow haired lad pulled over in a white convertible. one of the girls got in. his hand slid under her skirts and up her brown thigh. she had no panties on and she shifted her position so it was easy for him to get his fingers in and send her humping and whimpering and cursing in spanish. the girls stopped dancing. one of the boys was picking his fingernails w/a miniature stiletto.

i walked over to the radiator. someone had painted it over to match the rest of this crazy set up. my room was an eggshell of petrified steel, the breadth of a fingernail. unpenetratable. likewise i could not get out. i could feel the girl advancing out of my site line. each hair on the back of my neck was a razor. i felt her coming and hands unzipping the front of her sheath. her underwear was black and wired and her skin was creamy. i could feel her pliant nipples between my callouses. she removed her cuffs. there was a black stem poking like a feeler from the mouth of her sex. she plucked, popped, sucked and spit back the bing w/such graceful abandon that i greased my pants. i shoved my middle finger (hard nail) up her cunt then bent her in half. cracked her open like a party favor. a flood of objects spurted, exposed, then faded.

hard egg shapes the ovaries of a princess—white, all white, and speckled w/light. coke dispensers, drills bouquets and scores of trembling pigs on spits of white spike. purple and red cartoon rays outlined my hand. my fuck finger was still and brown. golden like the blessed shit of women.

her panties were slit at the crotch and had all the stations of the cross embroidered on the silk edge. she had truly been prepared for a night of love. her hips were oiled and her bust and twat dipped in merc and honey. her long legs (the inner seam) were dusted w/the powdery rouge of the poppy.
—carnival of souls.
—the lost icehouse
—highway of light
—beams
—headlights floodlights
the rays of traffic beckon like the hands of blake. pin-up babes in sweaters w/the masculine allure of lana turner. i was promised women and there were plenty of them. song on the radio:

frankie lee. there were plenty of them but i wouldn't have them. only one. she was the whole one. our synchronized sensations were a revelation; this girl in pumps w/the lips of a statue.

archway of womans arms. he advances. her thin blonde mane pulled back in a ponytail. they are advancing towards the old icehouse overgrown w/black plows.

eight figures of receivers were twisted out of natural in thick blocks of ice. some were naked and clawing. others were preening totally unaware that they were not encased in diamonds. they remained cellular and the block solid. my mermaid swished thru a warm channel and lay open and pulsing on the flat back of a floating fragment. ice-floe. a glacier and a fifth of jack daniels. and the reflection in the bottle was the dancing belly of a woman.

youth in fresh white shirt. girl underglass in a nest of white gardenias.he caressed the mounds of flowers and suddenly it was flesh heaving in a net of white mist. he was startled by union.the way their bodies locked predestined without hesitation.as if there was no question about their common worth.

the black tunnel.clouds of mink.a southern past of steam and melody.clouds of pink mink.nothing fascin-ated him more than the way a horse looked like a gun. he picked one up and slipped it in the mouth of the sleeping girl.as the shell burst so did the scenes she made and the parts she played.

k.o.d.a.k.
plea to george franju

picture this. I'll play the killer. 16 millimeter.
ebony and ivory. the purest contrast. iris closed.
open sesame. a screen of creamy white satin. on
that wedding lap a white persian cat. a pale hand
pets. milk purr. pan up slow. its me see. in a
black silk suit. dark glasses. kid gloves. as
sinister as the law allows. I've returned from the
opera. prowl cat tom cat. if I'm male it doesn't
matter.

I'm on the ledge. thats a several story drop.
how did I execute my brilliant cat walk? thats up
to you franju. but there I am. perched on her
window sill like a dirty bluebird. the back of my
neck is wet. I sit there what seems for hours.
a human chess game. she makes the first move.

its quite simple. she gets up to adjust her sloppy
stocking. her easter spikes could use some vaseline.
her matt gesture is reflected in black patent leather.
shoot to the ruffled vanity. mirror image.
look at the kisser gazing from that mica. lipstick
so thick you could carve your initials in it.

no alias not me. my initials are PLS and I'd be
pleased to leave my monogram. close-up shot
of my steady fist. I'm cool as menthol. the kind
of confidence one achieves thru an open nose.

cocaine. I can do it. watch me raise my leather
fingers. bluebeard itching for a fleshy white neck.
I strike. she's no match for me. the cold adhesive
touch of the octopus. I remove my glove.
struggle struggle. glub glub. she's gone.

as the opening credits roll up. the killer, swift
as an athlete, is escaping. springing
from roof top to roof top. racing against pyramid
shapes into the black seine.

search party music. the killer. 16 mm. black and white.
g. franju. with patti smith.

george franju. media me. shoot me on the kodak.
I'll do it for free.

mad juana

you play mad juana who goes mad when she looses her hand-
some husband. i play sonny bastard, the greece gigolo. you're
weeping. i waltz in and you can't help but note my teeth and
hair, wet and slick with glycerine. i take out a monogram
hankie from my sharkskin. i chloroform, but just a little my
poco. just enough to make you swoon to forget. all the better
to take you in my arms and run my hands down the front of
your house dress. mi amore i dig your floral print rayon. oh
pooh senorita your breast is missing a button. pop! pop! pop!
missing more buttons. swish! swish! missing altogether. ah-
hiayee! you feel the moji embrace against the stucco. i'm on
my knees lapping. your cunt is dripping chili beans. you
throw your head back. crack. you are so sentimental so hot to
trot. your rough red hands pull back my pommade. this is a
bull fight but i give up. seven enchilladas couldn't plug that
canal. bullseye on your heavy dimpled bottom and the bubbly
chicken skin of your thigh. yuka. now i see why you lose
handsome husband.

see me i split. i grip you by your grease ball ponytail. juana
loco. your gyrating jelly. i dip your face in enchillada deesh.
now you have red spaghetti hair. now you are as crazy as ever.
i leave you here. i take all your money. buy brand new car. fin
the end.

the salvation of rock

rock, like sculpture, is the solid body of a dream. is an equation of will and vision. the marble poacher pushes and tests the grain then strikes in the space and manner best accommodating his ultimate purpose. he is working from the akimbo plane. from the archery of angles. the chiseled tip of the arrow merges w/the target. pioneer ships bloat and explode. the universe is in/flamed w/the passions of man. streaking the sky is a chrome troller of remarkable speed and luster. the high cranial of mill pogany. 1920. polished brass. seventeen inches. no face no mouth no wall of speech. simply a head. a breathing helmet.

the headress is obsolete. and perhaps language, like this bitching reference, is also finished.

i am being paid to speak so i speak. elsewise i would create only for lust. the ghosts that surround vision are moving in. they are filling our craniums w/the dust of huts. adobes and aggies. genius is asleep in a cave of marble. over there on the stone base lies genius-lidless and heavy w/the smoke that snakes from the pipe/line of past glories.

it was brancusi who had the courage to crack and reconstruct the intelligent innocence of an egg. brancusi birdbrain? perhaps. thru mold and concrete he shot the perfect shape into rock. the hard gold thrust of a feather.

the shape of a feather is the essence of flight. indians, the true levitators, took this feather and another and others. above and behind their head they fashioned a bonnet of plane.

crazy horse had one such feather. with it he scratched the shape of a bolt into the knees of a dreamer. blue eyes reached out. blue eyes scoped further. blue eyes focused a rock—a smooth stone which he caught up in leather and tied thru his ear as a gesture of promise.

he that plunders pays. once he bent down to pick up a diamond. he was shot in the knee and his knee opened and streamed the tears and words of his people. he wept and pissed and attempted to abuse his spoil and recapture the language of the lost.

here he gripped his ear and the ear of his horse.

he rode very fast and the wind whistled thru his wound. he manipulated the pain and reinvented the cliff and the waterfall—the totem of the redeemed. he proved the hand that pulls positive raises. hear then the levitation of the rock is truly possible.

stoned in space. zeus. christ. it has always been the rock and so it is and so it shall be. within the context of neo rock we must open our eyes and seize and rend the veil of smoke which man calls order. pollution is a result of the inability of man to transform waste. the transformation of waste is perhaps the oldest pre-occupation of man. gold, being the chosen alloy, must be resurrected—via shit, at all cost. inherent within us is the dream and task of the alchemist. to create from clay a man. and to recreate from the excretions of man pure and soft then solid gold.

all must not be art. some waste we must disintegrate. positive anarchy must exist so that we may come to know and resist and grow beyond the ancient shape of a feather.

what is a hero?
— a silent indian
— a uranian guerilla
— a hard and heartless abstract expressionist
— or a little girl w/glasses

somewhere in america, in a certain state of grace,
he exists.
one who never sleeps except at light.
one who falls and one who fights.
one who salivates on the rock of right.

VI. CORPS DE PLANE

corps de plane

i

we came into this area quite accidentally. there was no over-whelming suspense, no compelling drama. we simply drifted over and landed. on sand. our vessel sunk very quickly with no sound. the others removed their shoes. i had none and walked ahead, alone. my companions took an alternate route into adventure and i never saw them again. i was alien, alone. with no misgivings or regrets. we landed like a dream so i allowed the future to unfold like the petals of a seductive and sinister flower.

gravity was with me. i barely touched ground. therefore the burning granules did not harm me, only made small rude pits on the bottoms of my feet. these i caused to melt away, like expiring goggles in the dunes. i couldn't bear the marring and pitting of my elastic feet. in the clouds the men were performing their dizzying escapes. bomber pilots going up in red smoke. the explosions descended into a breeze that blew up my skirts. several layers of khaki chiffon lifting and revealing the wanton muff of a flower.

i am armed with sweating memory. beads of information like cartridges on a leather strap. revolution is one of our most charming commodities and the sands respond. revolt and swirl beneath my feet. strain and wave in the shape of a long and lapping tongue. i could not speak. i was trained to give, not receive, pleasure. there i was overcome. glistening hairs of the desert were aggressively clogging my pores. i was stretched out. i was jamming with the experts. sucking with the fibrous rhythum of the sand. the sand, first intrigued, was soon involved.

ii

there was a distinct pain in my right shoulder. i could hardly bear it. overhead, men with glowing helmets, carved up the city on a flat easel. the tri-color sketch of the final divisions were only an arms length from the long funeral curtains behind which i was hiding. 3-D bi-planes in the distance. the men gathered by the window sucking their pipes and discussing the approaching craft. i reached for the plans. the pain was excrutiating. i bit down on a capsule. overhead was the syndicated formation of enemy planes. one of the adrenal people flashed and flooded the sky with light.

we were waging a war of aerial design. the simple symmetrics of the chromatrope were sent back to base for analysis. i was given the clipped black tube for the insertion of priority information. i was very tired. i was amazed and making it. free and naked. invisible runner breaking thru the front with the blueprint of the future wrapped in foil. i was given a coat of ribbons and kissed on the neck by the general. here i am alone in my tent with no servant nor invention of amusement. i have little use for the war games of man. what i was searching for was as singular as radar. a brother-a dead woman-a shirt of electric hair.

what does it matter what I say? it's what i think that counts. planes of the human body. formation of a glacier and the long thaw. desire for the word obliterates the image. once my face is removed i am free to plunge sans identity into a pure investigation into sound. sound. a condition so abstract that i can almost taste what it feels like to utter the letters of your name.

iii

there are three voices within one cool white voice. when any one of these experience ecstasy, pain, or is at the summit of certain and concentrative mania, i exorcise my right of telepathic pleasure pull.

when one is fucking someone else i cry a name softly and then my own over and over until i know i've gotten thru. sometimes it's a long and wrenching process. often instant success, but i get thru. i cannot be forgotten nor blotted out. likewise, when i am experiencing something to be shared, i leave a traceable space open for any three of the one to slide and come in. i am not beautiful but vain enough to attempt to conquer distance. and breathless sleep.

iv

i awoke. i tossed off the blush pads. my free eyes understood. the light made my eyes twitch. i was annoyed, violated. i was also the possessor of an enormous appetite. i mechanically pulled the long velvet tassle that was hanging to the left of me and waited.

moody, sullen, uncaring where i was, i entered into the game of the written. and it was written that i should awake here and with servants. indifferent, inimicable and a servant myself. a maid of the future.

jeanne darc

i feel like
i feel like shit
i need a
i need a drink
and not vinegar neither
i dont want to die
i feel like a freak
dont let me cut out
i wasnt cut out
to go out virgin
i want my cherry
squashed man
hammer amour
love me
live me
hour to death
what the hell
hour to death
am i doing here
am i ending here
hour of death
and i feel so free
feel like fucking
feel so free
feel like running
got no hair
weighing me
cut so close
scalp is nicked
look like shit
hour to death and i feel so free

hour to death and i feel so free
turnkey turnkey
play with my pussy
lick my little
scull bait head
get it get it
get it in
get the guard to
beg the guard to
need a guard to
lay me
get all the guards to lay me
if all the guards would lay me
if one guard would lay me
if one guard would lay me
if one god would lay me
if one god

jenny

jehovah had two offspring. two offerings in jesus and jeanne. jesus sprang from mary the virgin wife in labor. jesus was modest and so was his mother. they cast their eyes down when faced by the father. they are the meek and the key to the land. jeanne had descended from moses the protector and laborer who demanded gods face. the masked was borne into rock and revealed the back. jeanne, the daughter of god, opened her sight, rolling complete.

sometimes quite unexpectedly i gaze on the child i have brought on the world. i have never seen her nor do i expect to see by any more than the power of her desire. as for myself, i make my work known for her to find. i feel no need nor sympathy for her. i did not feed or clothe or nurse her. in her life of lives i have done nothing for her. i do not know her nor do i own her. to me she is the properly raised daughter of a spartan. modesty should be attached to the ones who would raise her. may she grow modest or true to a position of vision—and may love and sorrow go w/her.

all little girls you are my daughters and new little boys you are my sons. do what you do and do what you ought to. all little children you are my friends. a spartan must search s/he is a wanderer. do not take pity, it has happy end. giddiness happiness absolute love. so will it rend and so will it mend.

here is the belly the scars that you gave me. the spot above my wrist and the brown line and in here deep in my cunt a scarline like the nile and a fork a long Y like the tigris-euphrates.

you are the daughter of mesopotamia. this is your pleasure and this is your grief. death in life in the kingdom as jeanne,

or life again in the new world with yah. ways are all won-
drous. passage in grace and all states of disgrace. you were big
and filled w/health. your trauma of birth is the miracle of your
eyes. it is truth that makes them roll and rolling they are. grey
w/huge black luminous pupils. pearls and jet radiant w/sweat.
our skin is waxen and marble. it is not the stoned skin of a
martyr, but of a daughter blessed w/right. the right of birth of
a daughter of light.

now let me relate the tale of the scissor. it was scorned for its
destine of waves into sugar. the scissor was used for sculpting
the prisoner. it clipped to the scalp and made ready joan of
arc. the sharp point nicked her crown and opened a gland.

the birds were rushing in/formation overhead.
the women were leaping and licking their lips.
the old ones thru their heads back. dizzy ecstatic.
in the internal inferno etched in flame
the last words of jeanne
all claims of her father
thru the name of her
brother
jesus jesus
on the back of jehovah
racing thru paradise
on another planet called earth.

health lantern

i want you to be healthy. i want you to project the light of safe
keeping. i also want to be feeling all the destructive rhythums
in your body. i want your cough to disintegrate into sex. i
want you to fuck and fuck me w/the same insistency in which
you are fucked by your cough. i want to translate your cough
into a laugh and laughter into a gasp and gas into jet. i want
you to beat off in the ozone. cataclyme dangerous mountains.
scale the airways of andes. i want you to lay w/your face to the
ground. to eat dirt and make love and never cough again, so
that we may dig all regions and ridges and gather the remains
of all that inflames into the sack of the jaw.

hymn

we hadn't eaten in two days. we were entirely intoxicated. for me it was his presence, the alcohol and the glow of communication. i couldn't bear to fill up with anything but liquids while he was near me. neither of us was able to eat. i had a soft dose of hashish which i washed down with calvados. i watched his hand grip the slender neck of the bottle.

the hash was coming on and i couldn't function. he led me to the door and saw me to the station. i was trying to vomit but there was nothing in my stomach except for a few crackers. we made no plan of contact. the bus pulled away and some nuns skirted across the window. i got involved with the hem of their dresses—a perfect round of socket stitches. i didn't get a last glimpse at him. i was a human bomb, a greased and mushrooming drill. the bus was moving into a black hole. i didn't resist. i saw his face and relaxed and left. i was gone. when the bus landed the driver came and got me. the car moved slow and wicked through the dense fog. it was thick and wavy like the breath of a beast. i could smell jasmine. the monastery was up ahead. the silence and beauty of the tomb of charm. i couldn't talk, i was paralyzed. in the bathroom i threw up in a trash basket. i rinsed it out and caught my reflection in the mirror. it was him and only him etched and soaked in the muscles of recognition. i braced myself against the ledge of the window and watched the mulled turnings of the novices below. fragile monks with necks smooth and cool like the skin of a magnum. pink bubbles drifted from the mouth of the youngest, lying with his face against a rock. the other boys kept turning devout and burning and trilling a long gush of sounds and verbs that were easily transferred into a song of mutual love.

the nineth hole

love was on strike. we made no attempt to put our energies
into what is mutual. for a while we would spurt rockets out of
phone booths. shooting and separate, same time same sky.

we collided brutally one afternoon and then again in the eve-
ning. i was prepared for it, however. only a few hours before
he came to call i had stopped action and lay back on the chair.
wide white enamel with pillows of goose down. i was very
comfortable here, so like sherlock, i shook a smoke. pipe
dreamed into a long and fastidious solo. i pictured him and
quickly solarized the image into pulsation. here i was able to
establish a visual position as accurate and blooming as a pre-
cious end paper. it was easy to spin out from there on and on
from sun to sun.

i was slumped over in a silk kimono stenciled with the bird
arms of laughing girls. the room i was in was cool and light
and furnished modestly. a long low table, a prayer rug, a com-
fortable chair and two bird cages of white wicker. it used to
be, a long time ago, that love birds cooed and dreamed in this
place. it used to be, a long time ago, a base of magic tragic
words of love covering the walls were maps and photographs
of mosques and dancers in the temple of rust.

we hadn't spoken in a long time. we were colliding into cane.
we were fucking against the earth and spinning around and
out of the room into the street. he was such a wonderful danc-
er. we were turning in a dangerous rootless limitless space.
mad packs baited and bagged. no words. foam and static.

trying to get you by telephone. booth assaulted by alien forms
and poking comet skulls. smiling boy moving thru glass. bub-

ble toys rotating in kids space. boy on phone—"call your bluff" silk threats. network of spit. girl stoned and rolling disappears in white coat. boy on phone—"i'll meet you" and "no one cheats anyone" can't move door jam. mass attack—mad squirrels. skull showers. miniature skulls shattering. relapse of imagination. silver stammering. bubble toy enlarging and taking off into the night. remains of children flora and lost animals scatter. the small park is suddenly smaller. a hand covers my face. grey gaseous luminous hills. a hand reaching for the phone.

i'll meet you" phone spittle laboratory hand reaching for phone animal specimen in rotating baby toy.

i'll meet you" phone spittle and a network of signals. the booth glowing and shrinking. hand reaching for the instrument. "we're meeting" blue forms blue kidspace and loose balls taking off into the blue "we've met"

my eyes are realigning. we were taking off into the blue and stammering as son yeux. i look in the mirror. what is needed here is new logic for new sores. here i become one with the adrenal people—seekers of alternate truths.

lies are social reality, a disease that manages to rudely penetrate the chamber of emotion. remedy? cranium beam—up. into the tissue chute down through into the pool dipping and cleansing and playing around. brief suspension and nap time on a metal cot. shutting our eyes having a smoke and drifting back into the magical land of love and language.

the first leap (into the divine) is the leap of language held in/ bind and in/kind with belief and a shimmering swoop of sailor netting. the air is high as wire over the ancient tournament.

i'm in balance over it. around each ankle was a message en-
graved in chain. there had already been the leap into the dan-
gerous consuming pit beneath the pool of wire on the mental
plane. wings raged against the screen. the flame. the aura of a
scream. of god of sound. this is the cry of love which man de-
livers after much pain and labor. this is the fruitfulness which
makes man warrior.

after we spoke i wandered around the room. i sat down in the
chair. i sat there and had a smoke and waited for you to mate-
rialize in the flesh. there i was completely happy. there i was
in harmony with the warriors and the mother of nature. there i
was told that faith is the key.

i had a dream that we were in a movie theater together. we
took a drug and made-out and fucked in the movie. a tech-
nicolor revision of the first story that filled me with ecstasy. to-
tal recognition of total truth. i sat on you and we didn't move
at all, we communicated.

i was happy when you arrived. we held hands and walked on
the boardwalk toward the aging arcade—the gate of god. we
found a photo booth and had our picture taken. we waited for
a long time and finally from the slot came two little flowers. a
honeysuckle and a tiny tiger lily. one was my face one was his.
they were flowers too. clear faced. no discernible image just
the radiation of a certain knowledge. you put one in my but-
ton hole. one was already behind your ear. you said that's how
the sailors do it in france.

you left. a lot of people were around you. i watched you for a
long time. it was not until much later that i realized you had
left. i stood up and had to bend over fast. i had a terrible
cramp, i had to shit. i shit in the shape of a pipe. it made me

feel very clever. a glove, luminous and black posed on the edge of the table. the end of christine. it was an unexpected omen. i put the glove on and examined the button. mother of pearl. i made a silky fist then relaxed and lit my sebsi. it was unclean and i spat resin. i sat on the bed and removed a cigar box and a book from the overhead closet. in the cigar box there were photographs. christine in france christine at play. i found the one i was looking for. she was standing, sweet and forlorn in the rain in front of a deserted cafe. i crumpled it up and started laughing. i laughed til i cried then i laughed after. in the book there are some pressed flowers. in the book is my shepherd i shall not want.

there is my chair and there i am sitting. what
the hell i light a joint. we've been thru a lot
and we'll bend thru this. faith, joyous amorphous
will keep us together.
outside: the image of a mountain
outside: the image of a mole and king
outside: the image of a book
a diary of pain and sun

here in my chair i am smoking and traveling. an inspired
thresher on the mat of prayer. holes? i can go for hours.
in weaving even the leaves do not escape being part of
the track and line of our lives. here i dream us from
thread to thread. in this room of light and modest
furnishings is our life, an enormous tabriz.

thread

being away from you i have to feel you like some people feel god. projection from and to and in time. to spread around from the center of the son of mergence; the eye the essence of the eternal flame.

we connect and rush easily thru love and death. our kernel is hard and blessed. the foundation of the smooth barracks. i pass from house to hospital to void. it's my circulatory system. it's my rare and exquisite fortune of torture. your name fills me with wonder. sounds you transmit i decipher. in labor i chose not to see my creation nor attach name nor gender. only the sound of birth did i wish to preserve in my consciousness. my own sound was riddled with hard spickle. it became the rough edges of a piece of sculpture. the most base of a madam. an immense and speeding poon. no one to bow to. no one to blame.

i was sitting by the window holding your button. i wanted to sew it on your coat but i was out of thread. it was dark and rainy and the leaves were shiny. i decided to go out and gather some up in my skirt for our carpet. i wanted to work on the hand of a soldier folded in prayer but i was out of thread. i remembered that there was a roll of silk in a box somewhere. you had given it to me when we were learning language. we shared words as treasure hunters joyfully uniting to piece together a tremendous stroke of luck. it was already there to be found. i unwound the bolt and felt a certain vibe a word. the word was the missing name of god. the word was written in your percussive blood.

a fleet of deer

a year has passed. i know this because there are that many more lines in my hand. in the center of my palm is a spiral. if i stare at it long enough it starts spinning. i have not seen him nor has he called on me in any form. i go through the motions of each day living a brighter richer life in dreams. i am used to a parallel existence. i am no stranger to the twenty-four track. but lately. lately i feel the night. the weight. i can't concentrate. i take a walk along the river. i stop to rest and watch my reflection ripple and crackle and beam. but it is not my face. the other night i lay back and felt his face consume and reshape my own. i couldn't move, gravity was dense and in debt upon me.

the luxury of sleep, rare moments of intense involvement with the present through labor or pleasure or a phone call from a friend. the uncovering of a certain memory. i turned and he was there, waiting, on his motorcycle. the shock of seeing him as i see him—an angel—quick, silent and corporeal in the banal setting of cars, whores and danglers made me dizzy with jealousy. i opened my eyes. the milky slant of his eyes, lidless and blue and gone.

ii

i rummage through the closet. it takes a long time, but i finally find what i'm looking for. a sack of red skin. inside are the remains of my fortune: a jacket, a pipe and a heavy blue button. i recognize the button. it's from his blue coat. as real in my hand as a spoon or a guitar pick. it takes on the identity of flesh. i grip my pipe. a lion carved from white clay. pure and soft, hewn from the bottom of the mediterranean sea w/a stem of amber. amber for good health. the lion for gentle rule. it feels great in my hands, like the essence of a guitar. hard yet yielding. i have a long smoke within the confines of the huge double closet. i lean my head against the mirrored door and prop my feet on the door opposite. another mirror. in this way i can watch myself smoke. i can watch myself fall apart or simply disappear without care. i am a surgeon. the vigil of tongue and scalpel. i am able to dissect the warped and flowering mounds which make up my personalities. i am able to do almost anything but free myself from his eyes. from his ancient and sorrowful gaze.

as for my own eyes, i am unable to focus on anything. like a lizard i am disgraced with the stigma of two ways of watching. god i'm shot. i'm really tired. i look at myself with my left eye. here i am victim-maiden in prayer before illusion. here is discretion and forgiveness. on the right plane is a blue and bulging ball burning with the missive urge for immediate frontal attack. i detest everything weak. i am the military. i am the black poet in the cell fasting and laughing. there is no fear that i will hang myself here. it is well known that my scarf is reserved as a vestment of vanity.

i understand genet because i am his brother. i am weak and the exploiter of the weak. in life too i am a prisoner. free to act and freeze and kneel and enact my part in the smooth social order. in the play of life. all the world is a stage because we relate shell to shell. we relate by chewing fat wads of sweet gum, blowing legend bubbles and feasting on the words within. words scribed by the master cartoonist. all our gestures and rhythums fit in the pattern of social rule like the bits of glass shaping the harmony within the kaleidoscope.

but what if one rebelled? one jagged edge pulling itself from the mire of melody up into the tube and choosing to scrape and puncture the open eye of a predictable merger. what if one refused and another and still another one until we all came to grips with this wonder of true love? of rock and roll? there is nothing but dream. nothing save the real truce with light. the flash and flood light on the root of the true interior. life is a dream? life is life. dream on the other hand is somewhere else. the state of purity on which we have once collided. that space has alluded us. rare moments and sex, often self inflicted, through work or illuminated nightmare but seldom with another. seldom do the two eyes meet. seldom is brother revealed as brother or a vision as vision. in life on this planet.

iii

i shut my eyes. when i open them i am on the summit of a valley of pure gold. there is no glare. for the gold is dull and powder like the hair of death as she goes running through the forest traced by a fleet of deer. in the clearing they are grazing, devouring flowers. their slender necks laced with amharic tattoo.

i am reckless. i never do anything according to the rules. there is a kink in me as regulated as the clock on the stove. when i go in to inspect time i stop and lean against the sink. i dig my heels deep into the flesh of the linoleum or the crude mosaics adorning the floor of the arena of the bull. the bull. a huge, black and shining specimen. the handle of crete.

his hard hump accommodates the acrobat. the head of a pin becomes eye of spider. i have been deprived of communicating in english. i am the eye of the eagle circling the arena of life. i am the eye, liquid and sour, poked and sucked from the curious bird. trembling to express the inexpressible. filled with the objective lust of the archeologist. i crave discipline, self contradiction. i am incapable of plot. skin graph perhaps but not plot. we pray to break our fear of submission to sensation. to strap within the movement of the roller coaster. to give in. exhale. to scream. to offer up oneself to the sacred bull charging and tearing into the skirts of repression. to lift ourselves up to the greedy assault of the stranger. i would do it all. rape, morte. give in totally to the rhythum of his whims all for the rush of unveiling and comprehending just one letter of the ancient alphabet.

easter

29 years have come down like a crown
29 years i have risen and fallen

the body
the endless dunes
the glittering mineral salts
my being stark like a soldier
i cannot fast/i must eat eat eat
the chalky golden paws of a lion
i don't care about art anymore
passion will pass on thru the veins of the future
further than the plastic creations of man
i embrace thee madman spiker
and slammer of the graceless pieta
as the shroud it exists
only as marble to kiss
as a relic/just a relic
rather the kiss within
the stoned merging of the kiss of brancusi
this is a rather foolish art lesson
the history of art opened like a tomb of chain
alone in the study
in the luming vaults of the ancients
i would pour over plates of siennese madonnas
the languid primitives
the lilt and tilt of a modigliani
a mountain/a monument
giving rise to a pair of laughing eyes
an italian girl with green stockings rolling
i bend over her

she opens her fragile vestments
i open her belly with my tongue implanted with lasers

i am too anxious and ready to move
to fall in love
her purple scarf/the green silk hose
 exit the library
everything is something else
a mouth is the wound between her legs
 i violated her with my pencil
 the brush, the tip of my fingers
her pit was a canvas
the frescoes of florence
the porous skin of plaster saints
all of art seems pointless
one blurring photograph of an elusive face
or the face of christ straining in wax
and stone.
the rack/the rock
making love on a carpet
red and vibrant
the breath of babies
vomit and piss
on the face of a worthless tintoretta
where are we going to eat
devour and gorge each other's face
oh i would rather be understood as a flaw
in the belly of the most elastic ruby
than a perfect specimen sans sin and desire
i long for italy
a constant voyage of discovery
lying with knees open in naples
the sins of tuscany
the tentacle that treed me

from the boundaries of my terrible skin
desire unleashed in the suez crossing
we long for what we cannot love
here i long to sup on the gracious purple blooms
shooting from the swift teeth
of a crown of thorns
you press them to my lips
i dip into your subconscious
i want to cut your entrails
OUT
and wash them crystal
and wear them around my neck
the suez gate clicks
the nostril splits
the boy spits on his hands
and oils the neck of his instrument
w/the rich narcotic of her desire.
behind the curtain lurks art
like a knot in a stick
everything gradually connects
i crouch down and excrete
a mass of speckled clay
an oasis shape craft
the stenciled limb
peninsula
the sleeping canal
the mediterranean stretches
like your hand over my mouth
as you slash my knees and feet
w/your pewter thorn hewn
for the slow ritual of slaughter
in the trenches its war
porcelain faces chime
blue and shell like

victory is a drug
which we take together
in the trenches of war
women in black cars
women in dark glasses
what i don't see
is translated by god

VII. BABEL

chain gang

lingua is a ladder of communication
a concentrative communal chain of being
beaming to bleed the balloon
circling the highest legend

lingua leads to the fleshy folds
surrounding the pearl
which encases the word

the architect climbed lingua
greased and seduced the lustrous
concentrate
and placed the captive caption
between the teeth of his wife
the urn

he then translated the ladder
as the letter and law of power
this translation was then made
into a body
of motion, a vertical line.
a tower.

the materialization of an indestructible train
a tower of chain that would house the temple
that would hold the woman who held the word.

the plan of the architect to offer his wife
upon the shelf of the self
and between her lips
the tip of the shell
that entrapped the pearl
so to rend and retrieve
so she would have to be kissed by god
bride of god and receive beads
of thought wrought
from the vibration of the sound
of the word.

ii

she was a creature of miraculous stamina. her desire
was to move like evolution. not to suspect, but to
expect, the rising of the sun and her own rising. in
the morning she was the star of heaven. visible
ground. she was a planet. the light breath of venus.
she was the tomb of travel-a perverse and babeling
princess of process.

she had long been prepared for the grasp of gas. but
as she was straddled and mounted, so she did gasp.
her mouth quaked and she swallowed the beam of beams.
the creator caused her to spend by the force of his
finger. the pearl he dislodged and crushed into powder.
this he did sprinkle over the blueprint and blame and
the rock of the world. lingua was lapped and blown and
scattered into shimmering particles of matter.

iii

the architect was condamné à vie
a victim of the collapse of imagination
two silver balls ceaselessly slamming
expanding deflating he was no longer able
to control the current of his adrenalin
nor gather together thoughts into pattern
he was brother mush
procurer for sister slime
memory of a man on the masters trapeze
dizzy and ravenous-aware and not there

his wife was preserved in a phrase
degenerate dust

but not before she excreted a daughter
possessor of the key to a chamber of languor
a spinning crazy wanderer struck dumb
a dumb foundling...

the people still attempt to connect. some become
slaves to the post-relics of commune. what they
once had made behind their eyes they were now
fashioning with their hands. wordsmiths present
it in the shape of good luck. a knife. a maker. a
worker in metal. alchemists cracking the code
egg of babel.

so it occurred and so it goes on
miles of wire shaped like a chain
the oe of a shoe and the ou of a soul
dust of the word that shakes from a tale.

babel
(s/he)

art is committed thru the greed of the architect, the lust of a woman and the eye of a child.

1

a montage of experience. a man wakes up. it's 3 a.m.. he looks in the mirror and notices that his skull and temple has altered in the night. he has lost his confidence. there is famine in his shell. the fields that were fertile and greasy are covered w/ mist. he pops a goofball. if he lifts so will the dust. undercover is the true word protected by a layer of protective jelly.
—look at my face
—i recognize you
—my face has changed during the night
—i'm satisfied it's you
—i have no proof of this change
—i have no photographs of you
—we have no proof of anything
viz. we are not safe.

they descended from a breed almost totally extinct. everytime grace shot their picture would squint. the saddled macedonians and the elephants combing the long hair of their loved ones. shot after shot of another age. wandering forever over long sheets of ice. the ice age. and all ages devoured by the law of water.

2
(looking for howard)

i went to the fqih to find some answers. she set a crystal oblong on the brazier and said look down. unfolding in the wavy glass was a desert. i am on a donkey. regard! eternity! a girl on a donkey with a leather saddle.
- am i searching for something?
- that's it! cries the fqih.
i look back. the image remains the same. i long to knock up shadow, climb down a ladder and mount the donkey. unfortunately, it is forbidden. fate, like a slogan w/fervor, is a will that is written, filled out and sealed.

3

he was a painter blank and sick and finished w/the image. he craved new scenery, new conceits. he came to connect w/the supreme architect-the one who had fired the foundation of babel. the one who had passed the name of names thru the tongue and womb of a woman. she who had caused god to grind and sputter commandments of teeth and mango. avenger of eve. a moslem a motto.

the idea of this woman loomed like a portrait - wet and indiscreet, over his head. he was told that the word had been translated into the cryptic graphics of a celebrated dancer. a girl child of dizzying vision who was made to wander, scarred and veiled, dumb and eternal, over the earth.

so he was gripped w/the ghost of her. so he was determined to find her. thru the erotic stimulation of her genital orifice - her true mouth - he would seize and please her and trigger the speech and speechless within her. his palate was dry and he wanted a drink. he had all the necessary colors for the infusion of vision. he experimented and overexposed random women in the desert. all in preparation for her and toward the completion of his canvas of slaughter.

for awhile he dealt in the hotel care. he was the blackjack. the stationary point sur la table roulette. he was winning barge - he was in the chips. but it wasn't money, it was information he was after. rumors. pieces and whispers. in crete there was a woman who opened to no/one. for awhile the slick tar on her limbs and her ebony stick fan concealed that she was not like the others. she had been proclaimed a shock mute. yet still some claimed to have heard her singing deep and sweet, w/ an erect fan, as she bent bareback on the bull and sank wet and willingly into a planet of pitch.

this bitch he uncovered. and this bitch he did slit and scores of other daughters. holy whores and distorters of simple sensation.

—you seek wisdom
—i seek pleasure
still another death was a tongue. a soft and fertile root prickled w/the oily pale hairs of a seal. a lurking convenant. words received and words not spoken.

4

he wanted a drink. he entered the hall of sighs. it was a rock club. he paid the admission w/his hands. he shoved a sniffer of ice down the throat of the hatcheck girl. he leaned against the bar w/a fistful of glass.

—whose next? shouted media
—who wants to be a sign of the times?
he picked up his drink but before he could swallow he was obstructed and paralyzed by contact spewing from the mouth of danger - a dancer.

structure after structure. phrases like stairs. language as a ladder and he looks up. he stops time. but she is gone. he can still

censor though. he grips the rein and traces round the circular
stares and she is there. a vase. he shoves his fist in like greedy
monkey.
—there is room here to open my hand
—there is room here to spread my fingers
—look again. there is still room.
there is no obstruction. nothing. not even void. later he exam-
ines his hand. it has been altered one of a kind. covered w/
fiberglass. a fizz of insulation. he motions for her to remove
her face.
—his greed
—her spit
he grips her tongue and rips it rips it out. lavender forest. a
petal drying folding and incapable of speech.

5

woman one and on and on. failed alchemist. his existence
wept. yet he continued to search her out. the possessor and the
rose of the physical hieroglyph; a dance or diagram of sound
and movement. ancient egyptian profiles in rhythum. the pri-
mal position of the tongue synching in the myrrh of slow soil-
ing ritual.

6

there he became the obsessed archeologist. his nights were
spent bent over the cryptic scrawls on the lips of chosen
stones. searching for the word and the woman of the word. in
kenya the voice of his youth wrung from the call-cell of the
feminine one. rung after rung. he climbed down. he made a
pass at the guardian of the broken veil. he motioned to her and
breathed in her mouth. soft smoke a buzz of frankincense. she
returned his gesture with the odors of pleasure.

each hand cups a hill. she is now stretched on a grading glazed w/crushed robins egg. the pulpy gas pads are pressed against her heels pressing against a wall of tone and pressure. she is being prepared for the great bend on the back of the bull. her legs are wrapped w/pink satin strips. she slips into the sheen of a film concerning the limbs of la lyre.

apollo - broken arrow and wing of the offender. who is one who leaped onto the drawbridge of de chirico. who is one who prepared a glass of tea and restructured time and dance. who is one who caused a shadow over gog gate of god.

7

track indistinct. murmurs outside a discotheque. he removes his shirt. he adventures thru the long halls of an ancient building. he is exploring the inside of a desk of a great man. the breath of a renowned photograph. light pours thru the black venetians. a girl is doing upper body exercises. she is horizontal on the easter bar. her trainer stands dark and objective over her. her eyes roll up. overhead are the black venetians. within is the space and terrain of black venus.

in another room, another time, an old man lays down next to a young girl. she is slender and naked and perfectly still. she rises discreetly so as to let the gentleman, respected and enduring, assume his customary station against the wall.

after he had settled she thought of getting back into bed with him simply for the honor of his pure and silent exposure. for the sheer aura of lying limb to limb in limbo within the tomb of reverence.

she sat cross legged in the doorway dressed in a green slip. she was smart, pretty and very sleepy. she turned away and slipped off for a moment into the arteries of a monstrous foreign department store. bronze and empty. when she returned he was sleeping peacefully. he was covered w/fresh linen and over his eyes was a beauty mask of pale blue satin. she could not bear to disturb him. forgetting that she was immodestly attired she walked on thru the halls.

the dream that was unfolding before her was like destiny, yet not synonymous w/memory. she knew ahead was sweet excitement. she knew that allahs hand was behind her cradling her butt. his was a glove of greased celluloid gently prodding and molding her anal cavity. she felt herself give in to a plush bed of devils food. moist crumbs covered and jammed w/her flesh. there she was a gift. there she was another piece of cake.

8

he beckoned to her. she was standing in the blue field dressed in a cotton skirt and scant halter which emphasized the chiseled line of her sweetly oiled shoulders. he beckoned and then he beckoned to the men. they circled and flashed lasers of heat jetting and beating her oiled flesh w/sweat and bleaching her skin. the thirsty animals sterilized down her beads and tears and licked up the distillation of this precious excretion. lustrous oozing baroque. at night the juice rayed thru layers of tissue into the throbbing t/horny veins of their sex.

she advanced. the men, adorned in blue loin cloths, stalked. she advanced. they gripped her hips. mosaic of sky and flesh.

she was tense and gleaming in the sun. they split her open like a country. every man content w/his lot. they were very pleased w/the state of her mind. the estate of breast and of thigh. one gently prodded. one inserted a finger and played game upon game w/the underbelly of her sulky silent tongue. one punctured her waist w/needle teeth. one paints the tip of her tit w/ scented rouge.wood and charcoaled cunt. she was gently tweaked and kneaded. her torso was spread w/butter and pollen and parted just short of the arced position of pleasure and pain. they laid her on the table she had connected w/the inhaler. the needle was shifting like crazy. she was completely still. the gas traveled fast down thru the dorsal spine and down and around the anal cavity. the gas had inflicted her entire sphere w/all the elements of a voluptuous disease.

the green vapor made her feel light. she was a spinning, extinguishing bird of thread winging weightless and stateless thru all the stations of combe. the teeth slit the membranes and revealed the eyes of a lizard dotting the suspicious tongue. the eyes pearl regenerated - strove to connect the parallel visuals that would eventually evoke the final lusty words of power.

her tongue was the finger of a siren. they strapped it in w/ leather thongs. therefore, she could not scream as they fucked her. she looked up and laughed. she the victim? no! they the harem. the chimes were spinning. the hot breathing of the spectators made music. a sound trick. she welcomed it. she submitted to the magnetic core of the orchestra. she was a vinyl sweatbox. an imploding inferno. the scream she made was of a high pitch resulting in one long ecstatic aquatic contraction. pints of pure sensation. she started excreting. the coveted distillation of the eye of the lode-stone of the bottomless pit.

9

the wriggling membranes of remorse are absent. the crusade was not about discovery but escape. only he who wishes to pierce the voice of the flesh will drink from the cup. within the cup is a stream. he must sever his head and beam down in. now transposed he is no longer viking but a small girl. her eyes are big and sad and full of reproach. eyes possessing memories of queens and slaves and adventure. she opens her mouth and exposes a chilling verb reverbing loud and glittering laughter.

yet he also exists. they are twin nomads. in the icy space of promise she realigns her spine for him. vindication comes thru the comic rape of plague and regret. the ultimate match. the test of wit is dealing w/death itself. for this she is searching for this he is ready.

now that they have so collided his problem is no longer to find her but to keep her. seven skewer tablets arrange like cards for his face. wisdom is the cock releasing the pit of the vault. the leaves separate to reveal a woman in a rectangle. in order to keep her she has to be satisfied. her intelligence pride and primed like a canvas empty and stroked w/light.

10

he is scraping the attic. he must get thru. the country of the mind must have north light. a white and wide loft filled w/ space composed of air and brilliant rust. i watch him. i feel excited. i know what it tastes like to be a painter. i recognize the need for this space, so like him, i dog and claw and grasp.

there is nothing. nothing. not even a vowel. like crazy horse i am under oath to retrieve no spoils. once i forgot and once i was branded. once upon a time down thru time after time.

another room. i am eating goats cheese and mustard. on the table is bread and oil and all around me the fragrance of mint and pot. one cannot simply write a book. utter speech. one must discover something. i have no patience yet require to organize. rooms, windows, i keep building. i can never rest and repetition makes me nauseous. to build monsters. to hit the plunger and spray neo graffiti in the mouth of a river. to remember a word too sacred to remember.

11

he was on to something. he went back to the hall of sighs but it was boarded up. they repainted it and hung a sign over it. club yes. he had an idea she would be in there.
—you've been whirling round too many centuries.
—they are calling to me
heroes are milestones. she steps down. how could they bear to exist within this swarm of notes and wax w/out each other? he extends his hand. she steps down. he boils the water. she stuffs the teapot w/handfuls of mint. he prepares the glasses. w/the white handkerchief embroidered w/skaters she swabs a wad of raw honey from a pot of cones. he greases the glasses. in the background women are arched and screaming locusts. their heels are pressed against the wall in preparation for the rite of rites.

she is the model. she is a tulip bending and waving as lambskin electrobes vibrate her bud. he seizes her throat. he seeks

farther. he is making a painting. he has duplicated and extend-
ed the spiraling frescoes of giotto. over the cave she is also
spread. she, woman of crete, has taken the bull by the horns.

a flat surface. the ebony bull glistening w/sweat. the mounds
of red clay, wet and molding, beneath her feet. she would leap
from stream to stream. she bends down and presses her fingers
into it. emerging are the contours of a dream. a cinematic ter-
rain in primary colors. numbers balance above her shoulder.
her mouth is the mad fountain of a scientist. two photographs
wave thru space. one of a boy leaning against a reverb unit.
one of a fender head severed from the rest of the frame.
—she is crying ou
—she is crying where
she has been sentenced. death locks her forever in the face of
gods grace.

or perhaps it is the grave. she is delivered only as she is turned
to dust. there are no reporters at this trial save the film makers
of the future. over there is dryer and bresson. over there the
laundry turns. a frame of falconetti is juxtaposed w/the face of
one not yet shot - a high snap of jeanne d'arc.

12

in the archives of the forbidden cinema there exists a mech-
anism which can merge memory w/light and produce a sound
image of anyone existing in grace within film. there exists
another. the motion picture camera is the carving knife of the
collective. the kingdom of celluloid is common ground for the
whore and scientist. there exists another mechanism not yet
perfected. programmed for the retrieval of traditions action
b.f. (before footage). lie back and strap in. press your crown

and palms into the cream metal walls of a nuclear submarine. still in the brain is a freeze frame of a clipper ship. on the billowing sail is a watermark; an imperfection inherent in the clue and fiber of the cloth. it harbors within its bowels a cargo of damned and ancient moving pictures. the breast of aaron and the back of god shot by moses. close ups of the crucifixion. details of spike and the waxing feet of lot slipping thru censored districts of the city.

s/he is footage peeled from my brain.

she is an unstructured symphony racing thru the forest in a thin cotton dress. tiny jutting crystals loosen from her pounding feet. she has been fucked by donkeys junkies rock n' roll stars and servicemen. she is looking for a landing. a cast iron railing. she brushes past abandoned refrigerator boxes and overturned sinks.

everything is sinking in this mire. scum and algae. the quivering nostrils of plantlife. she commences her dance thru the junkyards and across the ribs of the water. her feet are splintered from rubbing back and forth over cracked bone. a station wagon overturns in the orchard. her miraculous ballet. the rise in her face. every phase of our being is incorporated in her fabulous useless movements.

13

the reputation of a dream. she lives up to it. loosening the robe of content she steps into the baths of the steppes leading down. it is white and still around her. her arms are veined violet and silver. it is the site of a small group of passage graves - the clava tombs - ringed by circles of stones, free standing and vibrant. she is standing in the center palming and raising a head outlined yellow.

boys w/flutes lose their footing and sink back into the command to wake up. their reeds vibrate a symphony of shrill demands. innocent pipes. micro-schools. cult of fishes. the children embrace her w/their eyes. they are cartoon guns. the auray which these pupils shoot penetrate the neon tubing the head in her hand.

the head leaps and rolls and strikes the boys dumb. they roll back and shoot the woman w/points.

not the singular wound per hand. but a constellation of small red points. it was fever. she was sweating silver ticks. she was lying on a table. he was standing over her. he manipulated her hot spots. her body was a discotheque which filled him w/violent sensations of warmth and eventually the eradification of his flesh into sound.

he caressed her hair w/his hands. his eyes were closed and he was moaning softly. her skull was resting in his hand and shinning like a superb walnut. rushing between their kisses were centuries of questions.
—are you despairing?
—why do you despair?
—i am searching
—i am searching
—i am knowing
—i know where

14

plot of our life sweats in the dark like a face. the exploding mystery of childbirth. of childhood itself. grave visitations. placid offers. what is it that calls to us? why must we pray screaming? why should not death be redefined? we shut our eyes stretch out our arms and whirl on a pane of glass.

an afixiation a fix on anything the line of life lingua love limb of tree the hands of he and the promise that s/he is blessed among women.

pinwheels

i was lying on the table. my neck exploded and my shoulders parted. a long shaft of energy realigned the jagged yearnings of my spine—a vine—which had been tenderly then violently manipulated by a mean and circular hand—a fathomless hand twisting me dry and hanging me up—washing me down and pounding me powder in the mortar of mourners.

century after century—from the divine apothecary—a human compound—a string of limestone tears—dispersed simutane-ously—past and future simulcast. so i made my way thru life after life. aware of dual poles while existing in the constant spinning present.

the room was empty. the master had withdrawn and i was alone. i was surrounded by plain. the other garden of eden. between parallel streams was the new tree—the night bloom-ing cereus—the queen of knowledge.
-the easter lily eagle claw
-living rock and barrel star
-little life and human ball.
i was waltzing on the edge of a stick. i was called upon to raise the challis of resin and partake of the blood and the reign of the cactus. loh-fof-oh-rah. the drug of time—of flesh tran-sported—thru flying and dying. euphoria. chosen of chosen. just like a dream.

something is crawling. its a lizard. no—its me. slithering rep-tile. all extinct bones are broken and from the hollow favors memory erupts. a reoccurring flash. something my subcon-cious is trying to remember. a girl w/ eyes like pinwheels. in-dependent eyes w/moveable lids. a child in/flux and forgot-ten. a child who wandered shamelessly into a city of vision and violence waving a space toy consisting of light weight vanes that revolved at the end of a pale stick.

up each nostril was a system of fragile bulbs connecting with a minute transmitter which served as a pupil regulator. her eyes were grey and flashing. they had a way of spinning and dilating. expanding in all directions. almond shaped and luminous slate.

I was lying on the table with my arms outstretched. there was a long period of radiance. of man and stallion merging statue. i was balancing the air on either side. the master entered. i could not stop him so i submitted to the flex of pleasurable torment.

life forces were glowing and charged.

there was an explosion. a crack. there was a field of children awaiting orders.
their eyes were pinwheels floating and spinning.
—children! shall we build a monument?
—invent sculpture?
—sure! they chimed.
they broke formation and realigned. they sat crosslegged in the high grass and sang the song of friedrich the levitator. he was the sun of the planet of love. he was the boy whose toys rose as he dreamed. sometimes he too would rise and wreak havoc and laughter along the land. one day the elders settled him down and reduced him to salt. one awakening grain trapped in a tear sliding down the cheek of a girl with polarized pupils. caught in her apron are snapshots which crumble into little paper balls apres view. a gentle archer. a tortoise. a

metallic weathervane. streets of meat and dormant strangers. bruised popsicles.

she sticks out her tongue. a glass cactus rotates. her vehicle—a sky device in the form of a revolving wheel of colored fire— hovers in tender skies. she is armed with love.she reaches out to clasp my neck. i resist and hold my breath and roll in a ball to the edge of a snow bank. i roll in a sea of warm vomit cleanser. i fall back in a cloud of concrete images and imagine my skull splitting like a brittle tootsie pop.

my face is greased w/the sweet scent of a baby blanket. in my nose is the taste of sugar.my skin is littered w/ a thousand snowflakes—gradually the entire storm. glass shapes kites and worms and little animals. leather bottles and secret messages.

someone brushes my face. a little girl w/ eyes like pinwheels. there is a desert in her cheek there is feather in the pigeon blood the wind is shooting/i rise from the table i take her face in my hands and kiss her on the mouth a kiss that melts like works in the night rushing milk pods of delight merging us in/ kind in the dark backword ghost dancing for the tribe of trial the tender simile of sun and smile.

comic warrior

AWAKE!
the forest is on fire. awake!
little dancing tree awake.
where i run so do create.
children do not fear. awake!

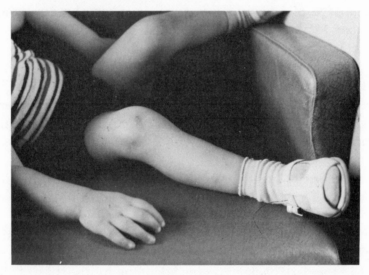

wake up! neo boy flashes down hill and valley
in his modal airplane bike. it's pale blue just
like his eyes and the sky and all who adore him.
he fills us w/energy and remorse as we watch
his crust be crushed into dust and witness his
death and fights right back to life. his ecstatic
pain. he leans against the grain and vomits and
stumbles and circles his heart. he's gassed and
the exhaust from the fumes of the fart he's just
laid lays him out. there on the hill w/his hand
resting on his chest lies the truth and test of an
age of shit. he's shaking and sweating and pull-

ing his jack. he's a gawdy cartoon man and
sometimes the moon or the stop of a bottle. ev-
erything is neo boy. the arm of your stereo. the
weeping of your child. how i suffer how i suffer.
the exhaustion - the tremor - the death of neo
boy pale as fire. rats gnaw and leap from the
birthday cake of neo boy laid to rest on a mira-
culous hook. forty odd swinging saints doing
choir boy twist stop and pay their fragments
and gnaw and wrap our hero w/ noir rubber tis-
sue. flamingo and coral birds flap his legs. yel-
low and screaming canaries are his shirt and a
cardinal is crown and bluebirds to trim then de-
file his organ of sound. neo oozes from pints of
shadow-blue and silver flickers of tepee light.
illumed cucumber and bird of hunger child of
paradise child of plunder. drenched in spiney
cockscomb waving down the wonder hair of the
florida river. he is fish by movelight. he is in the
hand clapped over the white bead of the coca
leaf. the handle of fender flag god and fan. he is
myth again in motive city he was dead he comes
again on a bed of slab he is rising reconstruct-
ing and soon to be conducting a universe of mu-
sic.

city of stars of glowing spears and sight city of
dreams and city of spice arcade city and city of
none. you were my savior and you were my son.
you are the unfolding guardian of tone-resili-
ent-elastic-sensory end. you are lifted down
from the hook. your flesh is strewn. i have no
time to mourn. w/ my thumb and thumb i grip
your jaw and palate and twist the sputtering

track and i crack your mouth open. oh my lovely
nut! i roll the prize in my palm and it cracks on
its own. a long golden tongue! flesh and blood
and beautiful to behold. mouth of a cave i could
kiss you forever. tip of a spoon and the seep of
your spit-comic warriors erupt from gold mean
as shit.

> sisters and brothers
> minature soldiers
> mongol hordes
> awaiting their orders.
> Yay! cries wavy deer
> Yay! cry all the toys

city of stars and city of boys. he climbs in his
jelly machine and switches the scene shooting
skylines of ticker tape and departing thru a
georgian curtain of orchids-splitting-refracting-
wet jet and cut jewels-very pale and very lovely
like a womans sleeping sex.

....

> "hooray I wake from yesterday"
> *jimi hendrix*

babelogue

i haven't fucked w/the past but i've fucked plenty w/the future. over the silk of skin are scars from the splinters of stages and walls i've caressed. each bolt of wood, like the log of helen, was my pleasure. i would measure the success of a night by the amount of piss and seed i could exude over the columns that nestled the P/A. some nights i'd surprise everybody by snapping on a skirt of green net sewed over w/flat metallic circles which dangled and flashed. the lights were violet and white. for awhile i had an ornamental veil. but i couldn't bear to use it. when my hair was cropped i craved covering. but now my hair itself is a veil and the scalp of a crazy and sleepy comanche lies beneath the netting of skin.

i wake up. i am lying peacefully and my knees are open to the sun. i desire him and he is absolutely ready to serve me. in house i am moslem. in heart i am an american artist and i have no guilt. i seek pleasure. i seek the nerves under your skin. the narrow archway. the layers. the scroll of ancient lettuce. we worship the flaw. the mole on the belly of an exquisite whore. one who has not sold her soul to god.

combe

already i am at the end.
is it not strange that i, a beam, should splay foot
a path so twisted and gridded. cut glass and barbed
wire. here i stalk, a wild and alien indian. here i
scoot thru the brush into the area of amalgamated
breeding. to the right an atomic energy plant
surrounded on all sides by an electric fence. over
the entrance is a sign not yet ciphered. it could
mean victory. it could mean danger.

men risk their lives. women give birth to the word.
a natural gamble in the hand of code.
code is the poetics of physics.
code is law and code is love.
a codeislam is a body of thought that houses illumination.
formed of the limb and the trunk of the tree.

i swing with sister in the context of a screened
porch. a girl w/glasses and braids and reading books.
her glasses serve not to strengthen but hiden her eyes.
i looked down at what she was reading. a system of
symbols covered w/wax. there were grainy close-ups
and covered plates. no. 41 was beyond description.
a hideous reptile w/eyes like windows. i flipped them
up and entered within them. there was a long path
leading to the black river. my sister was wading,
waiting w/the canoe. a sleek silver bullet over
the water, black and riveting as the image of the
future on a video screen. my sister was terrified
so i summoned the television to hover above us.

here she was able to identify, and thereby recognize,
her roots en route.

i am in favor of these united states. here is a land
baptized and broken. here are the rising foundations
for the spartan existence. the family will no longer
control the western hemisphere. it will exist in
its pleasure but not in its tyranny. our lungs -
window wings, will extoll the notes of a pure,
more powerful democracy intricate in its simplistics.
a leadership of snowflakes.

a child is watching a war movie. the bomber pilots
have a 50-50 chance and they know it. there is
nothing to loose. victory is on the other side of
boredom. i am watching the same movie. it fills me
with anxiety, agony. the moves of these brave faces
reduce my own adventures to the mere turnings of a
petticoat. what experience could i enter that could
compare to this?

when vision takes over one is in a state of grace.
one is a being pushed by the hand of promise. something
higher than adrenal-in takes over. these moments
do exist. one confronts the face or rides the back.
out of the hand feel the finger. out of the hand
and i start to whirl. out of the hand. one time i
lingered. and then i moved in another dimension. there
the hand cradled me. the slim limb straddled me. a wide
hard palm pushed me and the shadow that boxed me.
do you believe in god?
he is my trainer
the trainer that jesters me on. we have entered a new

period of gain. a new state of time. there are
contenders again and he has risen and thrown his
hat in the ring. and i am here too. lying small and
fetal in a center of a ring. radiating from my finger
there is a drone, a dream. there is a glowing parachute -
a way out. i am here and joyful to be so. here there
is choice. a system of action or action random and
terrible.

as a child i was graced with the gift of demateriali-
zation. i was also able to construct the scenes of
great mysteries. on the tip of my spinal tongue
was a pearl. the bait and calcium of the object
was discarded. the word pearl, however, was venerated
and catalogued. the creation of flora, fauna, emotion
and mineral was necessary inspiration for the creation
of the name—a word.
i am on the path. just another alien indian. things
are new to us and each artifact is carefully termed
and examined like the rump of a fresh cadet. the ribs
of the venetians kept us amused and pounding for several
hours. a tower. a butterfly. everything is absurd,
delightful. but the greatest thing of all is the
book. are the cryptic tablets—the tombstones of
sculptors. there is no existing translation.

to reinvolve ourselves we must face the past
with the existing spirit of the future. each day
i awake and a comb is lying on the pillow. it is
not mine. it belongs to margarita my ancestor. it
belongs to the time as experienced by the old city.

the comb i press to my scalp. i feel it relates
to the skull of the soul but it's function is not

coming in.
a coronet of stars
ornament of the tame
no one to vowel
to vow to
to blame
how did i die?
i tried to walk thru light
w/tangled hair
not yet prepared
for the valley of combat.

babel field

"we know how to give our whole life everyday."
                                                    a. rimbaud

wherein war is expressed thru the violent hieroglyphs
of sound and motion. a scream is a shoulder. the profile
of life. raised are our instruments—the lubricants
of aggression and flesh. a blade of glass thru the
vortex of sound. wound and winding bandages, are
distributed by boys posed before the spinal region
of the parthenon. the columns. words of sand - psalms
of love and guerre coursing thru our veins. we are
the adrenal people. we need action. words we use up.
grind into powder like sex and death. a progression
of sand modules - calcium grains irritating the smooth
throat of the sea of possibility. on the raft lies
one overthrown with a hooked jaw and blown ray gun.
the eye of the sun
the eye of the son
is washed w/blue fluid.
it is the father himself who removes the particle.
here we have the flaw in the wedding cloth. here we
have the awakening grain. here we have the ammunition
and the essence of art/rat. here we have the necessary
component of charm for the construction of the fourteenth
jewel transmitting the waves that leads to the gates
which are closed and shackled. violent compression
the abode of the blessed. only the thumb of the father
can undo the great lock or raise up the high tree.
w/weapons aimed high in akimbo we do so seek
said finger.

some of us serve as crusaders and some as flies
squashed against a fence. we live a spartan
existence. when we were seven the military swept
us away like merchants of venus and implanted with
us our instruments of battle.
what is art/rat?
self-crucifixion
high on the hills are the camps. high camps. high
tribes. 14 stations and beyond the rock a dream
of sound. beyond the throat of man there is a
violet claw stretching and scoping the distended
organ of god.
the tower is the symbol of penetration. there was
no actual structure save the image of two parallel
lines proceeded to point. the joint the prick the
finger the needle. the eye of the empire and the
emperor crowned w/communication. a peak hypodermic.
sometime of day god shoots up on it.
the count of nails chooses to straddle it.
and the daughter of god chooses to face it.
chooses to shoot it under the tongue.
the cross is just the true shape of a tortured woman.
forming and reforming and feeling the finger.
do you believe in god?
he is my trainer
i was trained to run toward a ribbon of tension.
attention! i was trained to run line and to selflessly
face and feed the front. on the cots the prostrate
soldiers screaming with no sound. writhing around
and pulling the rims of their ears like horns. there
was too much traffic too much pain i couldn't plug in.
i couldn't plug in anywhere so i hid my amp in the

bushes and threw my guitar over my shoulder. it weighs
less than a machine gun and never runs out of ammunition.
we were crawling thru the dunes. we slivered over the
hot mounds like coins. the grains, pocing our silk
camouflage, acted as irritants arousing our flesh.
words we use up.
only four remain
attached w/the symmetrical luck of a clover is love
and sex drugs and death. sound is the final analysis
of an equation involving X and intuition. sound is the
healing worm injected in the underbelly of the tongue
of love.
communication
w/heaven
is here man
the penetration
of the I of butter
sun butter which we dread and spread on our hair.
we grease and wage war w/fat roman cats
we fall on our knees
we jack on our strats
rings radiate from our ears distended skin trumpets
your opiate is the air that you breathe
and the ways that you manipulate your particles of charm
here i am an empty warrior
here i am stripped of ribbons
of honor and of rhythum
here i am utterly bruised by finger
here i am broken of figure of speech
i figure not to linger w/the finger forever
here i am reeling in and like a small fish returned.
here i am in taps on the field. sands are littered w/monuments.

w/guitar necks like bayonets. testaments of truce and
debt. i raise my guitar to the sky. i hold it in/pawn
with my two hands. i kneel and return to the note
of service. the scream it makes is so high pitched
that nobody hears save the herd of sound.
save the clowns of heaven
guiding the fold
and granting us wisdom
the kingdom of bliss
the lord is my shepherd i shall not want
me i just laugh i reel from my amp
the bush is in flames
but i could care less
i'm leaping lizard
leaping lizards
i'm in a hurry
i don't plug in
i'm at the finish
i'm finishing
i step up to the microphone
i have no fear

zug island

i know
all
your secret dreams
i know where
you are
goodnight
sleep tight
sweet streams
sweet beams
god light
you from
afar

list of illustrations

special appreciation to andi ostrowe, pclp